4

Savor the Tradition

DISCOVER BOAR'S HEAD

Savor the Tradition

DISCOVER BOAR'S HEAD

Photography provided by University of Virginia Host Properties, Inc. except where noted.

Photography: Cover, pages 50, 52, 63, 66, 73, 74, 77, 86, 92, 98, 108, 109, 111, 112, 113, 114, 127, 130, 131, 136, 140, 141, 142, 143, 150 © Mike Rutherford; pages 7, 50, 105, 108, 130 © Kristen Rose; page 84 © Thinkstock; pages 60, 91, 105, 119, 120, 123, 141, 142 © William Walker; pages 21, 47, 53, 56, 58, 103, 106, 110, 141 © MJ Arquette; page 102 © Gropen Inc.; pages 51, 55, 107 © UVA Public Affairs; pages 51, 104, 109, 132 © Jack Looney Photography; page 51 © Mark Portland; pages 54, 55, 56 © Mike Klemme; pages 64, 69, 111, 117, 134 © chrisdscott Films; page 112 © Meredith Montague; page 131 © Jen Fariello; page 132 © Ryan and Rach Photography; page 132, 133 © Meg Runion Studios; page 133 © Cramer Photo. Historical information researched and provided by 3 North. All additional photography copyrights, see pages 154–159

Published by

Historic
HOSPITALITY

An imprint of

SOUTHWESTERN
Publishing Group®

P.O. Box 305142
Nashville, Tennessee 37230
1-800-358-0560

Editorial Director: Mary Cummings
Project Editors: Alison Nash; Tanis Westbrook
Recipe Editor: Nicki Wood, CCP
Art Director and Book Design: Starletta Polster

Library of Congress Control Number: 2012945449
ISBN: 978-0-87197-574-4

Manufactured in Canada   First Printing: 2014   7,500 copies

Table of Contents

Foreword

At Boar's Head we fashion a welcome table from the tradition of hospitality and food prepared with a sense of place and the thrill of exploration.

We're inspired by the beauty and bounty of Virginia farmland, rivers and forests, as well as the culinary curiosity that drove Thomas Jefferson. His collection of herbs, vegetables, fruit trees and grapes revolutionized how Americans dined almost as much as his experiments with then-exotic foods such as ice cream and pasta, unknown to Americans of that era.

As a cradle of colonialism, Virginia transformed the early cuisine of the new republic. Based at first on English cooking techniques, colonial cooks altered their old ways with the New World ingredients they grew, gathered, and hunted. Gradually, European techniques combined with Native American and African customs, and the cooking of Virginia emerged a unique entity.

By the time Jefferson's cousin Mary Randolph wrote the first genuinely American cookbook in 1824, *The Virginia Housewife*, the new country had begun down a path toward a cuisine recognizable to modern Americans, based on familiar ingredients and grown on lands similar to those tended by Thomas Jefferson. Equally important to the cooking of the new country were Jefferson's culinary and horticultural experiments with vegetables like sea kale, orache, hot peppers, nasturtiums and Italian tomatoes. Jefferson was the nation's first culinary seeker, combining the familiar with a search for the unusual.

It takes skill to interlace traditional and new ingredients, to use conventional ingredients in updated ways, and to revive old recipes with novel ingredients. This has been the goal of the Boar's Head chefs, and they are pleased to share their craft with you, both in our restaurants and in your kitchen.

We hope recipes from Boar's Head lead you to prepare dishes with a sense of history and place, and the spirit of invention that is the spark of the evolving South. If our efforts inspire meals shared with a warm welcome and an open hand, the mission of *Boar's Head Cookbook* is complete.

We thank you for inviting the Boar's Head into your kitchen, and anticipate you'll be as sumptuously fed at home as you are in our resort.

Introduction

Discover Boar's Head, a unique resort filled with Southern charm, comfort, and character. Our classic Virginia resort, featuring 175 luxurious guest rooms on a 573-acre estate, is an exceptional destination for leisure, conference travel, and special events.

Boar's Head is steeped in history. Almost seventy years before Thomas Jefferson became President of the United States, the land on which Boar's Head and Birdwood are situated was part of a 1734 Land Grant and the site of Terrell's Ordinary. A hundred years later, Martin Dawson, a neighbor and financial advisor to Thomas Jefferson, and the first benefactor to UVA, built a water-powered grist mill on the banks of the Hardware River. In the 1960's this same grist mill was carefully dismantled and reused as the historic heart of the Boar's Head.

This magnificently bucolic world-class resort in Charlottesville opens its doors to you, offering unparalleled hospitality at the foot of the beautiful Blue Ridge Mountains.

Today, golfers walk the same hills that made Birdwood one of the most successful farming operations in the 1830's. *Tennis* Magazine rates the Boar's Head, with its twenty-six indoor and outdoor courts, as one of America's Top Fifty Tennis Resorts. In 2013, UVA's 33,000 square-foot McArthur Squash Center opened with 11 courts and spectator seating for 300. Our Fitness Center, with a full complement of equipment and trainers, can customize your workout or lead you in one of our 50-plus weekly exercise classes. Ask about our adventures programs, which include hot air ballooning and rock climbing.

Building on the lifestyle and beliefs of Thomas Jefferson that natural and preventive health was achieved through a daily regime of exercise, healthy eating, education and stress reduction, The Spa at Boar's Head has incorporated his philosophies into its signature products and distinct services.

With 22,000 square feet of event space, the Boar's Head is a place where meetings make history, couples make promises for a lifetime, social affairs make memories, and families build traditions.

Whether it's after a tennis match, a round of golf, a bike ride, a shopping trip, or a relaxing spa treatment, we invite you to join us for a memorable meal or event in one of our four restaurants and various indoor or outdoor venues.

Boar's Head is owned and operated by the University of Virginia Foundation.

Discover Boar's Head

Birdwood, August 28, 1917

oar's Head is steeped in history. Almost seventy years before Thomas Jefferson became President of the United States, the land on which the Inn and Birdwood are situated was part of a 1734 Land Grant and the site of a rustic inn, Terrell's Ordinary. A century later, Martin Dawson, Jefferson's neighbor and financial advisor and the first benefactor of the University of Virginia, built a water-powered grist mill on the banks of the Hardware River. The same grist mill was dismantled in the 1960s and repurposed as the visual heart of the Boar's Head.

A map of the most inhabited part of Virginia containing the whole province of Maryland with part of Pennsylvania [sic], New Jersey and North Carolina. Drawn by Joshua Fry & Peter Jefferson in 1751.

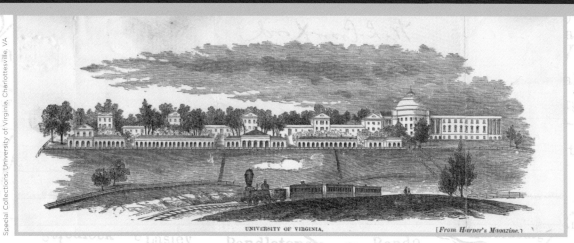

UNIVERSITY OF VIRGINIA.

[From Harper's Magazine.]

The University of Virginia. This print first appeared in an article called "Virginia Illustrated: Adventures of Porte Crayon and his Cousins," in Harper's New Monthly Magazine, *August 1856.*

Thomas Jefferson was inaugurated third President of the United States in March 1801.

The Boar's Head Inn, Charlottesville, Virginia

Eolus Mill was constructed in 1834 by Martin Dawson and Martin Thacker on Bellair Plantation.

Birdwood

Water Tower at Birdwood, constructed 1910

Barn and silo at Birdwood, August 28, 1917

The story of Boar's Head begins with the land on which it is built, land which is saturated with a historic legacy—a crown grant in 1734; centuries of country estate living and agricultural bounty; and ties with Thomas Jefferson and The University of Virginia. It is the land that became Birdwood.

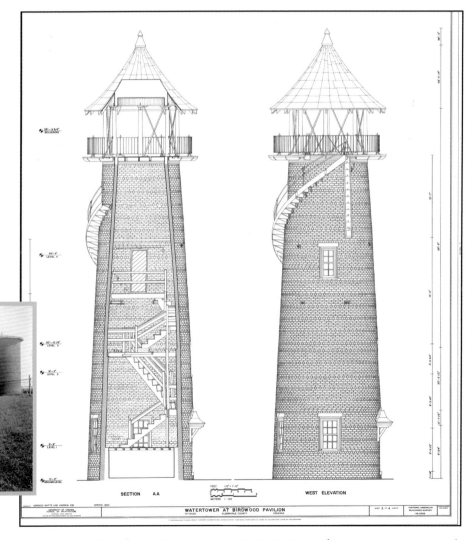

SECTION   AA   WEST ELEVATION

WATERTOWER AT BIRDWOOD PAVILION

Water Tower at Birdwood—designed by Hollis Rinehart (Birdwood owner 1909–1921)

The Beginnings

"I know of nothing so charming as our own country."

—Thomas Jefferson, 1788

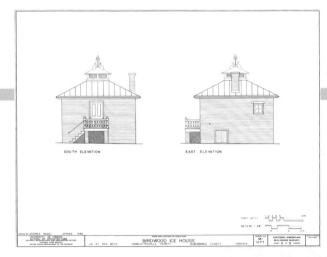

Ice House at Birdwood, 1819–1830

*Shadwell (Thomas Jefferson's birthplace) and Birdwood
depicted on map of West Virginia, 1908*

Birdwood, August 28, 1917

Land Grants

The Birdwood land has seniority and pedigree. The original Lewis-Terrell crown grant of 1734–35 is older than the United States, as is the original map drafted by Thomas Jefferson's father and Joshua Fry in 1751. Albemarle County, the location of Birdwood and Boar's Head today, was divided in 1761, creating two additional counties, Buckingham and Amherst. The Albemarle county seat was moved to Charlottesville, royally named for Queen Charlotte Sophia.

Special Collections, University of Virginia, Charlottesville, VA

Library of Virginia

The Lewis-Terrell crown grant—A 3,000-acre land grant to David Lewis Sr. and Joel Terrell from Secretary of the Colony and Colonial Land Office Patents. Terrell's Ordinary served as a resting place for weary early travelers.

Thomas Jefferson's father, Peter Jefferson, and Joshua Fry are commissioned to produce a map of Virginia by Lewis Burwell, the acting governor.

1734–1735

1751–1754

A Taste of History

James Kerr purchased the land that would become Birdwood in 1773 and lived there for over twenty years. In 1798 Thomas Jefferson helped his former student, Hore Browse Trist, lease and then purchase this land, which Trist named Birdwood in honor of his English ties and family friend, the Reverend John Birdwood.

To Roast Large Fowls

Take the fowls when they are ready dressed, put them down to a good fire, dredge and baste them well with lard; they will be near an hour in roasting; make a gravy of the necks and gizzards, strain it, put in a spoonful of brown flour; when you dish them, pour on the gravy, and serve them up with egg sauce in a boat.

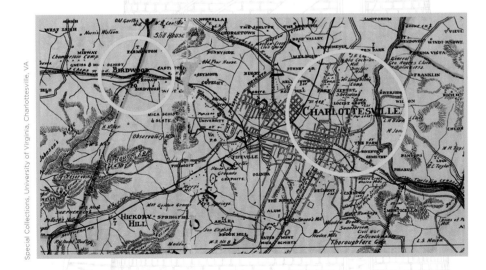

Special Collections, University of Virginia, Charlottesville, VA

Artist Jean Pierre Henri Louis
Hore Browse Trist (1775–1804) probably 1789/99
Yale University Art Gallery
Mabel Brady Garvan Collection

John Dabney buys 800 acres from Joel Terrell and David Lewis. Some of this becomes Birdwood Plantation.

James Kerr purchases 600 acres from John Dabney trustees.

Hore Browse Trist names the land Birdwood and purchases it from James Kerr.

1759

1773

1800

Prosperity

After Trist's death, over 400 acres of the Birdwood land was sold to Alexander Garrett, who later sold the property to William Garth in 1811. Garth, from one of Albermarle's most prominent families, turned Birdwood into an estate, one of the foremost country seats in the county. Garth's house, likely built by Jeffersonian builders, shares several commonalities with Monticello.

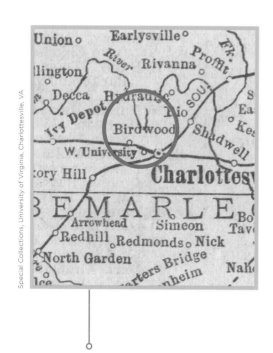

Alexander Garrett sells Birdwood to Thomas Garth, a prominent landowner in Albermarle County.

Thomas Garth gives Birdwood to Jessie Winston Garth, one of his sons.

Jessie Garth sells Birdwood to his brother, William Garth in 1818.

William Garth builds Birdwod, his plantation home.

1810   1811   1818-1830

Garth owned Birdwood for forty-three years, during which time his family grew to include eleven children and his estate produced abundantly. Due to his interest in scientific advancements in agriculture, he founded the Hole and Corner No. 1 Club, which met every month to share the latest land conservation and crop production ideas.

The Hole and Corner No. 1 Club met monthly to share the latest on land conservation and crop production.

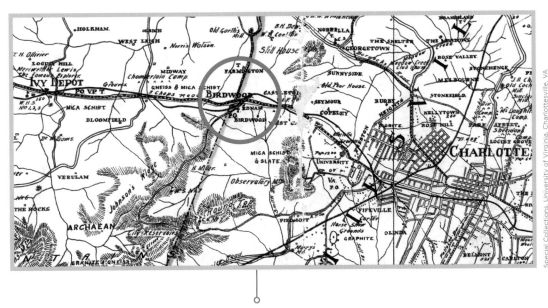

Special Collections, University of Virginia, Charlottesville, VA

William Garth founds Birdwood Jockey Club.

William Garth dies and leaves Birdwood to be divided evenly among his heirs, including his eleven children.

1827

1860

The Civil War Years

In 1865 Birdwood was touched by the Civil War. According to Ada Pyne Bankhead, granddaughter of William Garth, Union scouts disguised as rebels seized Birdwood, preparing it for an occupation by a Union regiment. After pillaging the mansion's contents for three days, General Sheridan marched past Charlottesville, sparing the University and the records in the clerk's office. Ada's grandmother received notice at that time that two guards would be sent to guard Birdwood, with the hope that "his men would no more disgrace the uniform they wore."

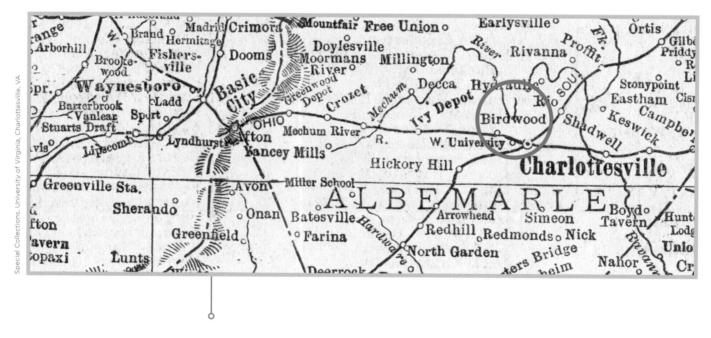

Special Collections, University of Virginia, Charlottesville, VA

The Battlefields of Virginia.
Detail showing Birdwood.

The Jesse Union Scouts seize Birdwood, use it for the Union Regiment for three days, and pillage its contents.

1861–1865

1865

In 1875 ownership of the Birdwood house and property passed by auction to Willam Stuart Bankhead, great-grandson of Thomas Jefferson and son-in-law to William Garth. Afterward, various owners—William C. Chamberlain, Edwin O. Meyer, and Charles Edgar—bought and sold parcels of the estate. Meyer built a magnificent Colonial Revival home named "Ednam" in 1901; Chamberlain added land parcels and a sizable addition to the mansion. Edgar sold 785 acres to Hollis Rinehart in 1909.

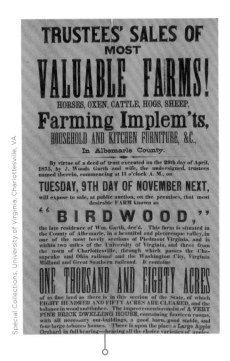

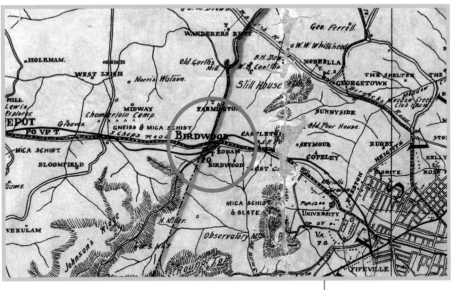

The Birdwood house and property (1,080 acres) is auctioned and sold to William Stuart Bankhead, the great-grandson of Thomas Jefferson.

Birdwood is sold to William C. Chamberlain.

William C. Chamberlain sells Birdwood estate to Charles Edgar, who adds a large addition to the rear of the mansion.

1875

1891

1903–1907

The Social Era

Hollis Rinehart, owner of a civil engineering and construction company, made additions and improvements to Birdwood, including a 175-foot water tower in the form of a lighthouse, a swimming pool, and the creation of several large rooms to house large receptions. In 1921 the Rineharts sold Birdwood to Henry L. Fonda, a vigorous and progressive proponent of the livestock industry who raised award-winning show horses and Hereford cattle on the property.

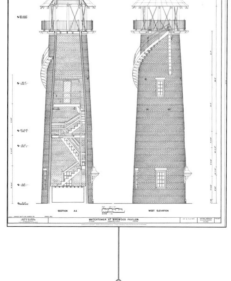

Charles Edgar sells Birdwood (785 acres) to Hollis Rinehart.

Hollis Rinehart builds a 175-foot water tower in the form of a lighthouse.

Rinehart adds a swimming pool to Birdwood.

1909

1910

1910

The year opened with a magnificent reception at Birdwood hosted by the Hollis Rineharts.

—John Hammond Moore, Albemarle; Jefferson's County, 1727–1976.

A Taste of History

Pound Cake

Wash the salt from a pound of butter, and rub it till it is soft as cream—have ready a pound of flour sifted, one of powdered sugar, and twelve eggs well beaten; put alternately into the butter, sugar, flour, and the froth from the eggs—continuing to beat them together till all the ingredients are in, and the cake quite light: add some grated lemon peel, a nutmeg, and a gill of brandy; butter the pans, and bake them. This cake makes an excellent pudding, if baked in a large mould, and eaten with sugar and wine. It is also excellent when boiled, and served up with melted butter, sugar and wine.

Rinehart alters the mansion to house large receptions, making Birdwood the center of social activity.

Reproduced from the 1920 *L'Agenda* with permission from Bucknell University, Bertrand Library, Special Collections/University Archives, Lewisburg, PA.

The Rineharts sell Birdwood to Henry L. Fonda.

1917   **1917**

Gardens and Grounds

One of Henry Fonda's aunts commissioned Virginia's preeminent landscape architect, Charles Gillette, to create a Virginia garden for Birdwood. Plans included a color rendition, a blueprint copy, a general layout plan, a planting plan, and a general detail plan that included a design for a formal ornamental entrance gate to the property, inspiring the current landscaping.

Fonda's Hereford cattle win awards at the Chicago International Livestock Exposition, 1921.

Fonda's two aunts, the Misses McCleery, live at Birdwood with him.

Fonda's horses win ribbons at Madison Square Garden in New York City.

Charles Gillette (1886–1969), landscape architect, produces one drawing and four blueprints for gardens at Birdwood.

1921   **1928-1929**   **1929**

The gardens at Birdwood are an example of Charles Gillette's classical "Virginia garden" style.

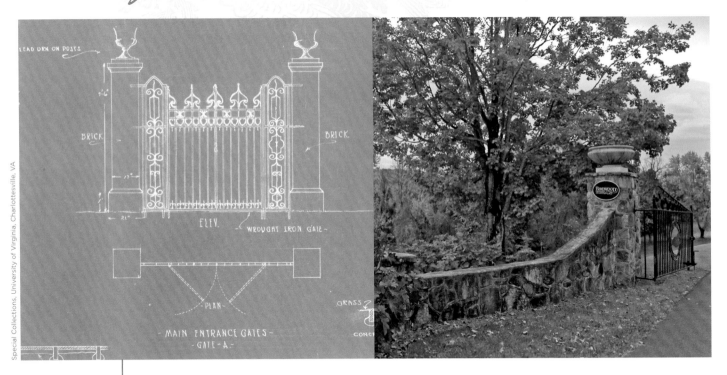

Special Collections, University of Virginia, Charlottesville, VA

Gate design from Charles Gillette, Birdwood general detail plan.

Henry L. Fonda sells 560 acres of Birdwood, "the greater portion of a tract of some 671 acres" to J. De Witt Wilde and his wife, Bessie H. Wilde.

The Wildes sell their 560-acre Birdwood property to Cornelius W. Middleton. He makes extensive improvements and adds modern conveniences to the house.

Cornelius Middleton and Isabelle H. Middleton sell a 550.469-acre tract of their Birdwood property (excluding the main buildings and about 9.5 acres) to Birdwood Estate, Inc.

Birdwood Estate, Inc., sells the 550.469-acre tract of Birdwood property to The Rector and Visitors of the University of Virginia.

1929   **1936**   **1966**

Birdwood, view from the Water Tower, August 28, 1917

Birdwood, center hall, November 21, 1917

Birdwood, enclosed porch, November, 21, 1917

Birdwood, view of Water Tower in the landscape, 1910

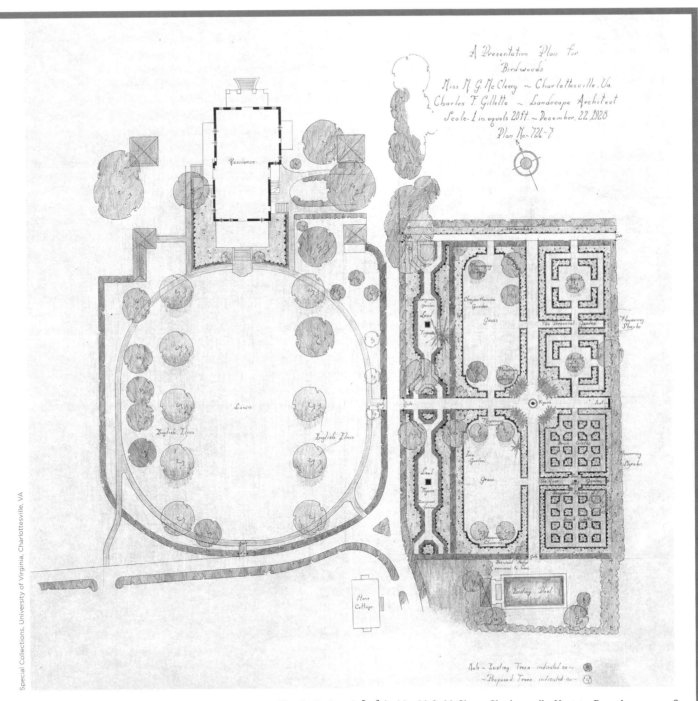

Charles Gillette, A Presentation Plan for Birdwoods [sic] for Miss M.G. McCleery, Charlottesville, Virginia, December 22, 1928

Thomas Jefferson

University of Virginia, Rotunda and Pavilion X (right), c. 1830

Thomas Jefferson, born in 1743 into a planter family in Albemarle County, was wholly committed to all things Virginia. With indefatigable energy and individualistic spirit, his life's work as a writer, statesman, ambassador, President, inventor, architect, author, botanist, farmer, and cook was infused with his love for his commonwealth—her landscape, her people, and her potential. He devoted his life to enhancing the incredible bounty of the state, whether in writing *Notes on the State of Virginia*; experimenting with imported fruits, trees, flowers, herbs, and vegetables; testing recipes from his travels abroad; or attempting to produce wine. The home he designed and the university he created embody his creativity and ideals as surely as his eloquent writing created the architecture for the new country he served as its third President. His legacy stands today and touches, in some way, every facet of Boar's Head's commitment to Virginia as well.

The White House

Shadwell (Thomas Jefferson's birthplace) in Albemarle County, 1908

The Architect

AUTHOR OF THE DECLARATION OF
AMERICAN INDEPENDENCE OF THE
STATUTE OF VIRGINIA FOR RELIGIOUS
FREEDOM AND FATHER OF THE
UNIVERSITY OF VIRGINIA.

—THOMAS JEFFERSON EPITAPH, 1826

Special Collections, University of Virginia, Charlottesville, VA

Special Collections, University of Virginia, Charlottesville, VA

The University of Virginia Rotunda, 1895

Monticello, 1825, by Jane Braddick Peticolas
© Thomas Jefferson Foundation at Monticello,
photograph by H. Andrew Johnson

View of the West Front of Monticello and Garden Monticello. Jane Pitford Braddick Peticolas, 1825

Politics and Presidency

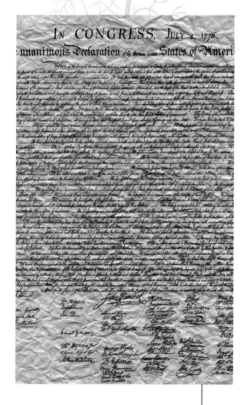

Rough draft of the Declaration of Independence, 1776

Jefferson submitted his "rough draught" of the Declaration on June 28. Congress eventually accepted the document, but not without debating the draft for two days and making extensive changes. Jefferson was unhappy with many of the revisions—particularly the removal of the passage on the slave trade and the insertion of language less offensive to Britons.

Thomas Jefferson, born in Shadwell, Virginia, April 13, 1743.

Thomas Jefferson authors the Declaration of Independence.

The signing of The Declaration of Independence.

Thomas Jefferson publishes and includes a map based on his father's Fry-Jefferson Map of 1751–52 in *Notes on the State of Virginia*.

1743　　**1776**　　**1776**　　**1781–1783**

Jefferson was the first president to live in the White House after his first election as president in 1801. During his term, Jefferson oversaw the Louisiana Purchase, effectively doubling the size of the United States. He also commissioned the Lewis and Clark Expedition to explore the northwest territory.

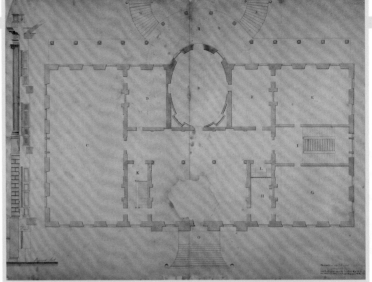

Washington: President's House (plan), 1792, by James Hoban
Thomas Jefferson Papers: An Electronic Archive. Boston, Mass.:
Massachusetts Historical Society, 2003

*Benjamin Henry Latrobe's first floor plan for Jefferson
shows a plan for a south portico with broad veranda.*

Thomas Jefferson, inaugurated third President of the United States, March, 1801.

The Louisiana Purchase was a land deal between the United States and France, in which the U.S. acquired approximately 827,000 square miles of land west of the Mississippi River for $15 million.

Thomas Jefferson inaugurated President for a second term on March 4. Thomas Jefferson, Medallion Portrait. Gilbert Stuart.

1801

1803

1805

Life at Monticello

Monticello was Jefferson's great love and, in a sense, laboratory. His interests connected Palladio's architecture to European cuisine and the latest labor-saving inventions, including ice cream and pasta machines. Here, he constantly rebuilt and improved the house, grounds, and gardens, experimenting, documenting, and planning even the smallest details of domestic life.

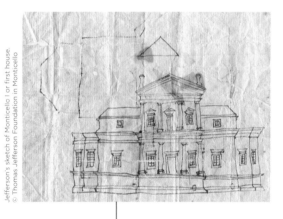

Jefferson's sketch of Monticello I or first house.
© Thomas Jefferson Foundation in Monticello

A Taste of History

Ice Creams

When ice creams are not put into shapes, they should always be served in glasses with handles.

Vanilla Cream

Boil a Vanilla bean in a quart of rich milk, until it has imparted the flavour sufficiently—then take it out, and mix with the milk, eight eggs, yelks and whites beaten well; let it boil a little longer; make it very sweet, for much of the sugar is lost in the operation of freezing.

Raspberry Cream.

Make a quart of rich boiled custard—when cold, pour it on a quart of ripe red raspberries; mash them in it, pass it through a sieve, sweeten, and freeze it.

Elevation of the first Monticello, 1769–1770.
Thomas Jefferson. Ink on paper.
Image Credit: Thomas Jefferson Foundation
Copyright © Thomas Jefferson Foundation, Inc.

American Treasures of the Library of Congress, Library of Congress. "Jefferson's Recipe for Vanilla Ice Cream." 1780s

1769–1770

1780s

"All my wishes end . . . at Monticello."

—THOMAS JEFFERSON, 1825

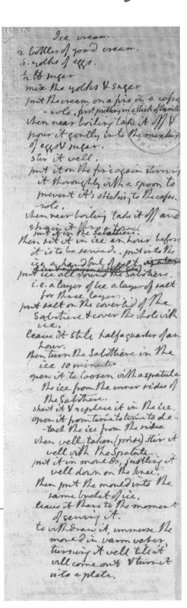

The first recipe for ice cream
recorded in the United States
is in Jefferson's own hand.

A leaf from a garden book of Thomas Jefferson.

Thomas Jefferson retired from presidency
and public life to Monticello.

The University of Virginia

Retiring to Monticello after two years as President, Jefferson conceived and designed the University of Virginia, an "academical village" embodying his architectural and educational ideals.

The cornerstone of the University's first building was laid in 1817, with Thomas Jefferson, James Madison, and James Monroe in attendance. The first class entered in 1825, and the first degree was conferred in 1828.

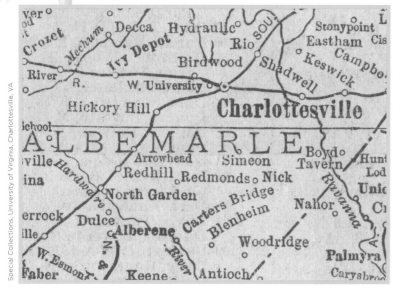

Special Collections, University of Virginia, Charlottesville, VA

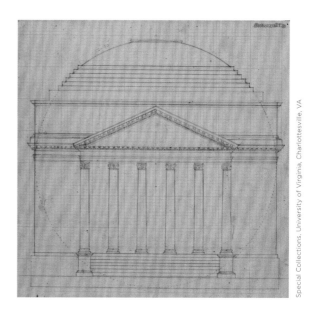

Special Collections, University of Virginia, Charlottesville, VA

The University of Virginia "academical village" is conceived and designed by Thomas Jefferson.

The cornerstone is laid for Central College, which will later become the University of Virginia, on October 6.

1811

1817

> *"I hope the University of Virginia will prove a blessing to my own state, and not unuseful perhaps to some others."*

—THOMAS JEFFERSON, 1825

Thomas Jefferson

Special Collections, University of Virginia, Charlottesville, VA

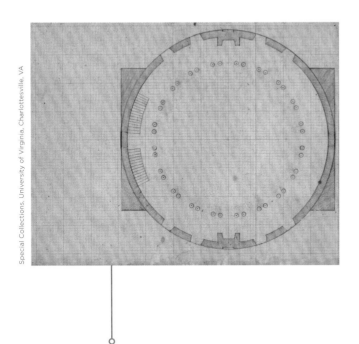

Thomas Jefferson's drawings for the Rotunda.

Thomas Jefferson founded the University of Virginia in 1819.

Nicholas **Philip** Trist marries Virginia Jefferson Randolph, grandaughter of Thomas Jefferson.

1819   **1819**   **1824**

Open for Classes

The University of Virginia opened with eight faculty members and sixty-eight students. Jefferson could not have guessed the scope and prestige the current university would attain or that his plans for the university campus would become one of the most influential planning and architectural ideals in American history. Boar's Head is now owned by the University.

Special Collections, University of Virginia, Charlottesville, VA

Jefferson's grave marker
© Thomas Jefferson Foundation at Monticello, photograph by Mary Porter

The University of Virginia opens for classes with eight faculty members and sixty-eight students.

Thomas Jefferson dies on July 4.

1825

1826

"*I have been planning what I would shew you: a flower here, a tree there; yonder a grove, near it a fountain; on this side a hill, on that a river. Indeed, madam, I know nothing so charming as our own country.*"

—THOMAS JEFFERSON, 1788

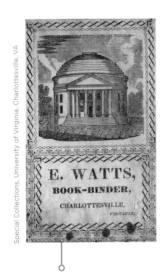

Special Collections, University of Virginia, Charlottesville, VA

Special Collections, University of Virginia, Charlottesville, VA

E. Watts, book-binder,
Charlottesville, Virginia.
The earliest known printed
image of the Rotunda.

Reverend Martin Dawson leaves a portion
of land from his Bellair estate, the first
land donation, to the University of Virginia,
making Dawson the first in a long legacy
of benefactors.

This lithograph shows the University of
Virginia as it appeared in 1856.

1827

1835

1856

The Rotunda Redesign

The Rotunda Annex was completed in 1859. When it burned in 1895, Stanford White of McKim, Mead, and White reconstructed the Rotunda as an elaborate Beaux Arts interpretation in the Roman style. In an effort to expand the library as well as emphasize the ceremonial space of the Rotunda, White increased the height of the dome room by eliminating the entire middle floor of lecture rooms, widened the skylight, and replaced Jefferson's slender double pillars with large single columns with Corinthian capitals. He also added a portico on the north face of the Rotunda and utilized new building methods to improve the durability and fire resistance of the structure. The building remained this way from 1898 to 1973.

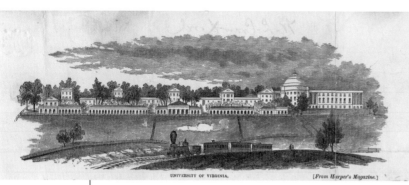

UNIVERSITY OF VIRGINIA,   [From Harper's Magazine.]

The University of Virginia. This print first appeared in an article called "Virginia Illustrated: Adventures of Porte Crayon and his Cousins," in *Harper's New Monthly Magazine,* August 1856.

1856

The Rotunda Annex catches fire due to faulty wiring. All but the brick shell of the Rotunda burn in the fire.

1895

In Stanford White's 1896 Rotunda redesign, shown here, a two-story library filled the dome. Today's design replicates Jefferson's two stories, with an elegant Dome Room on the upper floor.

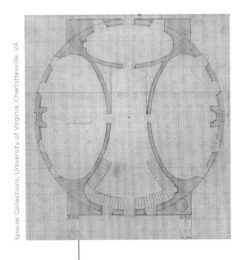

Stanford White of McKim, Mead, and White reconstruct the Rotunda after the fire as an elaborate Beaux Arts interpretation in the Roman style.

The original Dawson's Row buildings, built in 1859, are demolished; they are replaced with new buildings, which continue to bear the Dawson's Row address.

1899

1950

Boar's Head Inn

Original grist mill timbers were used in reconstruction of Old Mill Room at Boar's Head.

In 1834, a century after the original land grant, Martin Dawson, a neighbor and financial advisor to Thomas Jefferson, built a water-powered grist mill on the banks of the Hardware River. Dawson died a year later, but his bequest of over 538 acres to the University of Virginia made him the first of many benefactors and was used to fund dormitories bearing the name "Dawson's Row." The mill operated as "Family Mill" and later as Eolus Mill; however, its immortality was assured when John Rogan used the relocation of the mill to preserve and transform the treasured Virginia artifact. The old mill was carefully dismantled and reconstructed piece by piece as the historic heart of his quintessential Virginia inn—Boar's Head.

Eolus Mill was constructed in 1834 by Martin Dawson and Martin Thacker on Bellair Plantation.

The Builders

"We feel better when we find ourselves in the presence of the past . . ."

—BRENDAN GILL (1914–1997), AMERICAN ARCHITECTURAL CRITIC

The Cover, The Boar's Head Inn Brochure, c. 1965

The Boar's Head Inn Brochure, c. 1965

Changing Hands

Walker Timberlake purchased the property on which Dawson's mill was located, renaming the mill "Family Mill" and operating it until 1863. It was later bought by Richard Hancock Kluge, an Ellerslie Plantation horse breeder, and renamed Eolus Mill. The mill escaped destruction during the Civil War. Although Eolus was "Keeper of the Winds" in Greek mythology, it is more likely Hancock's fascination with a horse named Eolus was the source. The mill later became part of the tradition and history of the new inn, where its history embraces new traditions and a unique sense of place.

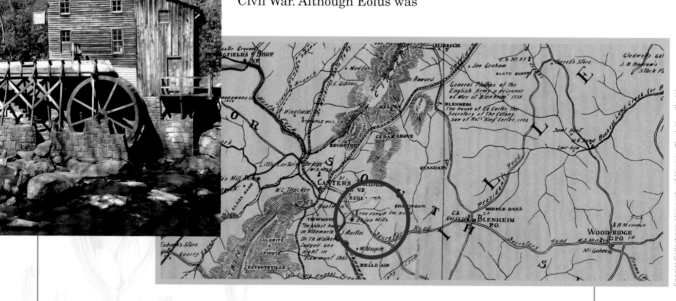

A water wheel grist mill is built by Reverend Martin Dawson and Martin Thacker.

Walker Timberlake purchases the grist mill from the Dawson estate and renames it "Family Mill."

"Family Mill" is purchased by Richard Hancock, who renames it Eolus Mills.

1834

1843

1875

"Today the Old Mill Room is graced with the time-worn timbers of the original mill . . ."

—The Boar's Head Inn brochure, c. 1964

Original stockholders of Boar's Head Inn development team, c. 1964. Back: John Rhea, E. Thornton Tayloe, Daniel van Clief, T. K. Woods, John Rogan. Front: Robert N. Flood and Bruce Sherme.

John Rogan at Boar's Head Inn site.

The inn's sixty rooms vary in price from $10 for a double to $34 for a suite per the Boar's Head Inn Brochure.

1964   **1963-1964** **1964**

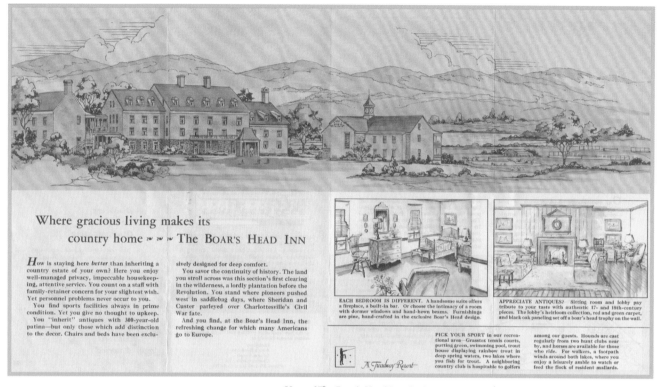

Where gracious living makes its country home ~ ~ ~ The BOAR'S HEAD INN

*H*ow is staying here *better* than inheriting a country estate of your own? Here you enjoy well-managed privacy, impeccable housekeeping, attentive service. You count on a staff with family-retainer concern for your slightest wish. Yet personnel problems never occur to you.

You find sports facilities always in prime condition. Yet you give no thought to upkeep.

You "inherit" antiques with 300-year-old patina—but only those which add distinction to the decor. Chairs and beds have been exclusively designed for deep comfort.

You savor the continuity of history. The land you stroll across was this section's first clearing in the wilderness, a lordly plantation before the Revolution. You stand where pioneers pushed west in saddlebag days, where Sheridan and Custer parleyed over Charlottesville's Civil War fate.

And you find, at the Boar's Head Inn, the refreshing change for which many Americans go to Europe.

EACH BEDROOM IS DIFFERENT. A handsome suite offers a fireplace, a built-in bar. Or choose the intimacy of a room with dormer windows and hand-hewn beams. Furnishings are pine, hand-crafted in the exclusive Boar's Head design.

APPRECIATE ANTIQUES? Sitting room and lobby pay tribute to your taste with authentic 17- and 18th-century pieces. The lobby's heirloom collection, red and green carpet, and black oak paneling set off a boar's head trophy on the wall.

A Treadway Resort

PICK YOUR SPORT in our recreational area—Grasstex tennis courts, putting green, swimming pool, trout house displaying rainbow trout in deep spring waters, two lakes where you fish for trout. A neighboring country club is hospitable to golfers among our guests. Hounds are cast regularly from two hunt clubs near by, and horses are available for those who ride. For walkers, a footpath winds around both lakes, where you enjoy a leisurely amble to watch or feed the flock of resident mallards.

View of The Boar's Head Inn, looking southwest, The Boar's Head Inn brochure, c. 1965

"Dining is an art in the Old Mill Room"—The Boar's Head Inn brochure, c. 1965

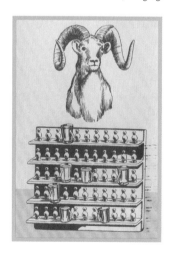

Detail of The Boar's Head Club, The Boar's Head Inn brochure, c. 1965

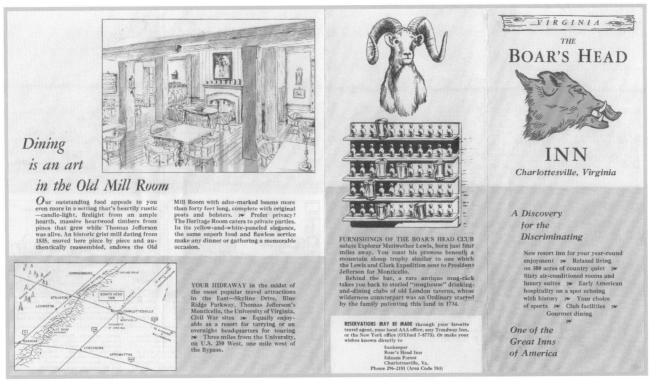

Dining is an art in the Old Mill Room

Our outstanding food appeals to you even more in a setting that's heartily rustic —candle-light, firelight from an ample hearth, massive heartwood timbers from pines that grew while Thomas Jefferson was alive. An historic grist mill dating from 1835, moved here piece by piece and authentically reassembled, endows the Old Mill Room with adze-marked beams more than forty feet long, complete with original posts and bolsters. ✒ Prefer privacy? The Heritage Room caters to private parties. In its yellow-and-white-paneled elegance, the same superb food and flawless service make any dinner or gathering a memorable occasion.

YOUR HIDEAWAY in the midst of the most popular travel attractions in the East—Skyline Drive, Blue Ridge Parkway, Thomas Jefferson's Monticello, the University of Virginia, Civil War sites ✒ Equally enjoyable as a resort for tarrying or an overnight headquarters for touring ✒ Three miles from the University, on U.S. 250 West, one mile west of the Bypass.

FURNISHINGS OF THE BOAR'S HEAD CLUB

salute Explorer Meriwether Lewis, born just four miles away. You toast his prowess beneath a mountain sheep trophy similar to one which the Lewis and Clark Expedition sent to President Jefferson for Monticello.

Behind the bar, a rare antique mug-rack takes you back to storied "mughouse" drinking-and-dining clubs of old London taverns, whose wilderness counterpart was an Ordinary started by the family patenting this land in 1734.

RESERVATIONS MAY BE MADE through your favorite travel agent, your local AAA office, any Treadway Inn, or the New York office (OXford 7-8773). Or make your wishes known directly to

Innkeeper
Boar's Head Inn
Ednam Forest
Charlottesville, Va.
Phone 296-2181 (Area Code 703)

VIRGINIA

THE BOAR'S HEAD INN

Charlottesville, Virginia

A Discovery for the Discriminating

New resort inn for your year-round enjoyment ✒ Relaxed living on 300 acres of country quiet ✒ Sixty air-conditioned rooms and luxury suites ✒ Early American hospitality on a spot echoing with history ✒ Your choice of sports ✒ Club facilities ✒ Gourmet dining ✒

One of the Great Inns of America

The Boar's Head Inn brochure , c. 1965

Guest room and suite, The Boar's Head Inn brochure , c. 1965

Sitting room, The Boar's Head Inn brochure , c. 1965

The Inn Opens

When the Boar's Head Inn opened, it offered two dining experiences: the Old Mill Room and the Heritage Room. The Old Mill room was described as *"heartily rustic . . . with massive heartwood timbers from pines that fell while Thomas Jefferson was* *alive."* The Heritage Room was more formal, paneled in yellow and white, and catered to private parties. The Boar's Head name is a symbol of hospitality. The image of a boar's head was first used on the signs of taverns and public houses during Shakespeare's time in England. The original Boar's Head Inn was famous for the warm welcome and good food it offered. This same tradition continues today at the Boar's Head Inn in historic Charlottesville, Virginia.

The Boar's Head Inn,
Charlottesville, Virginia

There were many social functions in the Old Mill Room, at the Boar's Head Inn.

Thirty-one guest rooms are added to the Inn. View from the north of the Main Inn and Hunt Club.

1965

1970

" . . . heartily rustic—candlelight, firelight from an ample hearth, massive heartwood timbers from pines that fell while Thomas Jefferson was alive."

—THE BOAR'S HEAD INN BROCHURE, C. 1964

Dating back to the 1960's, the Trout House has a rich history as one of the oldest buildings on the property. Purchased along with the land of the inn, it began as a spring house located on the water source connecting the upper and lower ponds. Once construction began, the decision to keep the house was made due to its attractive appearance. The spring house eventually became the "Trout House" in order to provide a unique activity for the resort guests. The house was stocked with trout so that guests could bring down nets and fish for their dinner. As a result, the Boar's Head became well-known for its trout dinners and the distinctive appearance.

1970

Letter discussing the 1986
Bacchanalian Feast

The BOAR'S HEAD INN
Ednam Forest
Post Office Box 5185
Charlottesville, Virginia 22905

Executive Office

Telephone 296-2181
Area Code 804

March 18, 1986

TO: MRS. ROGAN

FROM: GARY TORRENCE

I guess it is about time that we start discussing the
1986 Bacchanalian Feast.

Enclosed are some preliminary ideas. Please let me
know which items you like so we can set up a taste
test date . . . and I will work on the accompanying
vegetables, more precise and appropriate wording,
etc.

The BOAR'S HEAD INN
Post Office Box 5307
Charlottesville, Virginia 22905

Telephone
(804)296-2181

BACCHANALIAN FEAST

1989

MULLIGATAWNY SOUP

4" SOUP SAUCER
FRENCH LACE DOILLY UNDERLINER
SOUP CUP
MULLIGATAWNY SOUP - (6 oz.)
PARSLEY - CHOPPED FINE - SPRINKLE ON SOUP

PATE' POISSON

7½" GLASS PLATE
LEAF LETTUCE UNDERLINER
PATE' - #20 SCOOP - (1) EACH - CENTER
LEMON TWIST WITH PARSLEY SPRIG - (1) EACH - 12:00
CAPERS - (½ oz.) - 4:00
CHOPPED RED ONIONS - (½ oz.) - 8:00
SOUR CREAM & CREAM CHEESE SPREAD -(2)EACH - (½ oz.) ROSETTE - 3:00 & 9:00
CHERRY TOMATO - HINGED - (1) EACH - UNDER PATE'
BLACK OLIVE - (1) EACH - BESIDE CHERRY TOMATO
TOAST POINTS - (2) EACH - 1 AR 10:00 & 1 AT 2:00 - AT SERVICE

TOURNEDOS PERIGOURDINE

DINNER PLATE
BEEF MEDALLIONS - (2) EACH - (3 oz.) EACH - ABOVE 6:00
PERIGOURDINE SAUCE - (2 oz.) - OVER BEEF
TOMATO FLORENTINE - (1) EACH - BELOW 12:00
WATERCRESS SPRIGS - LINED TO BORDER EACH SIDE OF PLATE

STUFFED CAPON

DINNER PLATE
CHAMPAGNE SAUCE - (2 oz.) - ON CENTER OF PLATE
STUFFED CAPON WITH FIG DRESSING - SLICED THIN - (3) EACH - MEDALLIONS -
                                              SPIRAL ON SAUCE
JULIENNE CARROTS - (3 oz.) - LINED TO BORDER EACH SIDE OF PLATE
PARSLEY SPRIG - (1) EACH - ON CAPON

Menu for the 1989 Bacchanalian Feast

Winter Wine Preview Dinner
Saturday, February 16, 1985

Timbale of Chesapeake Crabmeat, Lobster and Spinach Mousse
McDowell Fumé Blanc,
  McDowell Valley 1983

Virginia Hunt Country Rabbit Soup
Landmark Chardonnay,
  Sonoma 1982

Roasted Quail stuffed with Artichokes and Wild Rice
Kiwi Regale
Schug Chardonnay,
  Napa Valley 1982

Grenache Sorbet
(McDowell, *McDowell Valley 1983*)

Interlude
  Ballroom Foyer

Wellington of Beef Tenderloin
with Duxelles of Piedmont Shiitake
Sauce Bordelaise
Zaca Mesa Cabernet Sauvignon,
  Santa Barbara 1981
McDowell Cabernet Sauvignon,
  McDowell Valley 1980
Columbia Cabernet Sauvignon,
  Yakima Valley 1981

Belgian Endive and Watercress Salad
Strawberry Dressing
Albemarle Goat Milk Cheese
Schug Pinot Noir,
  Carneros-Sonoma 1982

Frangipane and Pear Tart
Columbia Johannisberg Riesling,
  Washington State, Cellarmaster's
  Reserve 1983

The Boar's Head Inn
Charlottesville, Virginia

Wine Preview Dinner menu, 1985

The Boar's Head Inn, 1965

Savor the Tradition

Boar's Head continues the traditions of hospitality and fine Virginia dining—most especially those reflecting the bounty of the gardens at Monticello and historic Jeffersonian nuances—by incorporating the finest local ingredients and Virginia vintages into our widely hailed contemporary cuisine. As we celebrate over a quarter century of AAA Four Diamond Awards, we invite you to savor these traditions with us and to create your own with our master chefs and in the company of family and friends.

Birdwood Golf Course is designated a Certified Audubon Cooperative Sanctuary.

Hot air balloon
rides are a
tradition at
Boar's Head.

*University of
Virginia football*

Turkey Trot—
5K to raise
funds for the
University
of Virginia
Childrens's
Hospital

Birdwood Hospitality

For many visitors to Charlottesville, including our guests, their first view of Boar's Head is the Birdwood property. Today, golfers walk the very land which was Birdwood while Boar's Head visitors and University of Virginia students enjoy athletic facilities and amenities for golf, tennis, and swimming. The Starters and Salads recipes in this chapter honor the first-in-place legacy of Birdwood in Boar's Head history, as well as taking their usual place at the beginning of delicious meals served here.

Birdwood Estate, Inc. sells the 550.469-acre tract of Birdwood property to The Rector and Visitors of the University of Virginia.

Birdwood becomes an executive conference center for The University of Virginia. Various pieces of art appropriate to the era of Birdwood are displayed from the University of Virginia's Bayly Art Museum.

Birdwood Golf Course, developed by The University of Virginia and designer Lindsay Bruce Ervin.

1967

1979

1983-1984

*Birdwood is designated a Certified
Audubon Cooperative Sanctuary.*

—AUDUBON INTERNATIONAL CONSERVATORY, 2003

UVA HONOR SYSTEM
RECYCLING PLAN
IF LOST ONE - TAKE ONE

The University of
Virginia Honor
System, Birdwood
Golf Course.

Birdwood Golf Course is designated a Certified
Audubon Cooperative Sanctuary. The certification,
bestowed by International Audubon, is based upon
a consideration of the natural environment of golf
courses as an ideal setting for wildlife sanctuaries.

Birdwood is listed
on the National
Register of
Historic Places.

1984   2003   2003

Birdwood Golf Course, developed by the University of Virginia and designed by Lindsay Bruce Ervin.

2012 renovations to Hole 3.

Sweetheart Martini

Makes 1 drink

3 ounces cherry vodka	1/2 ounce maraschino
1 ounce vanilla vodka	cherry liquid
1/2 ounce Triple Sec	1 strawberry

Shake the ingredients with ice in a cocktail shaker. Strain into a martini glass.

Pear Martini

Makes 1 drink

3 ounces pear vodka	1/2 ounce Triple Sec
1 ounce vanilla vodka	2 ounces pear nectar

Shake the ingredients with ice in a cocktail shaker. Strain into a martini glass.

Irish Kiss

Makes 1 drink

1/2 ounce Irish whiskey	Whipped cream for garnish
2 ounces Irish crème	Green crème de menthe
1 ounce vanilla vodka	for garnish
1 ounce chocolate liqueur	

Shake the liquors with ice in a cocktail shaker. Strain into a cocktail glass. Garnish
with whipped cream and crème de menthe.

Lobster Salad Cocktail

Makes 4 servings

1	cup mayonnaise	1	teaspoon minced chives
1	tablespoon Dijon mustard	1/2	cup diced cucumber
Dash of cayenne pepper		1/2	cup diced red bell pepper
1	teaspoon fresh lemon juice	1/4	cup minced shallots
1/8	teaspoon salt	1/2	cup diced tomato
1/8	teaspoon white pepper	1	cup diced lobster meat

Combine the mayonnaise, mustard, cayenne pepper, lemon juice, salt and white pepper in a medium bowl and mix well. Add the chives, cucumber, bell pepper, shallots, tomato and lobster and mix well.

Spoon the lobster salad into stemmed cocktail or martini glasses. Garnish with micro greens. Serve on cocktail plates decorated with orange slice halves, edible flowers and greens.

Lobster Cakes with Mango Vinaigrette

Makes 8 servings

2¹/₂	cups fresh corn kernels	4	dashes of Worcestershire
¹/₂	cup Creole rémoulade sauce		sauce
¹/₂	cup mayonnaise	1	egg
¹/₂	cup diced red bell pepper	3	cups diced lobster meat
¹/₂	cup sliced green onions	1	cup panko
4	dashes of Tabasco sauce		Salt and pepper to taste

Preheat the oven to 350 degrees. Roast the corn on a baking sheet for 5 minutes. Let cool, then chill. Combine the rémoulade sauce, mayonnaise, bell pepper, green onions, Tabasco sauce, Worcestershire sauce and egg in a bowl and mix well. Fold in the corn and lobster. Add the bread crumbs and mix gently. Let the mixture stand for 1 hour. Shape ¹/₂-cup portions of the mixture into cakes. Arrange on a baking sheet. Bake at 350 degrees for 12 to 15 minutes. Drizzle with the Mango Vinaigrette. Garnish with micro greens and/or cilantro leaves.

Mango Vinaigrette

2	tablespoons Dijon mustard	2	cups vegetable oil
¹/₄	cup mango purée	1	cup apple cider vinegar
2	tablespoons sugar		Salt and pepper to taste
2	tablespoons tarragon, chopped		

Whisk the mustard, mango purée, sugar and tarragon in a bowl. Whisk in the oil and vinegar alternately in parts. Season with salt and pepper.

Melon Salsa for Oysters

Makes about 2 1/2 cups

1 cup finely diced cantaloupe	2 tablespoons cilantro leaves, chopped
1 cup finely diced honeydew melon	1 garlic clove, minced
1/4 cup finely diced green bell pepper	3 tablespoons fresh lime juice
1/4 cup finely diced red bell pepper	2 tablespoons rice wine vinegar
1/2 jalapeño, finely diced	1 teaspoon olive oil
2 tablespoons finely diced red onion	1/2 teaspoon ground cumin
	Fresh oysters on the half shell

Combine the cantaloupe, honeydew melon, bell peppers, jalapeño and red onion in a bowl. Add the cilantro and garlic; toss lightly to mix.

Whisk together the lime juice, rice wine vinegar and olive oil in a small bowl until blended. Whisk in the cumin. Add to the salsa mixture, tossing to coat. Taste and adjust the seasonings, if desired.

Serve over fresh oysters on the half shell. Garnish with lemon wedges.

Roasted Vegetable Crostini

Makes 12 crostini

Roasted Vegetables

1/2 cup diced zucchini

1/2 cup diced yellow squash

1/4 cup diced red onion

1/2 cup diced eggplant

2 tablespoons chopped herbs

1/4 teaspoon chopped garlic

1 teaspoon salt

1/2 teaspoon pepper

4 tablespoons olive oil

Crostini

12 baguette slices

4 tablespoons olive oil

Assembly

6 ounces goat cheese

Micro greens or fresh
cilantro leaves

Preheat the oven to 350 degrees.

For the roasted vegetables, combine the vegetables, herbs, garlic, salt, pepper and olive oil in a bowl and toss to coat the vegetables. Spread over a baking pan. Roast for 10 to 12 minutes. Let cool. Maintain the oven temperature.

For the crostini, brush each baguette slice with the olive oil. Bake for 5 minutes or until golden. Let cool.

To assemble, top each crostini with 1/2 ounce goat cheese and about 2 tablespoons roasted vegetables. Garnish with micro greens.

*Eggplant and squash were grown in the original
vegetable gardens at Monticello and team here with the freshly
baked bread served at Boar's Head during every meal.*

Tostones with Braised Pork Belly and Pickled Onions

Makes 20

Pickled Red Onions

2   red onions, sliced
1   cup vinegar
1   teaspoon salt

Dry Rub

1   tablespoon cumin
1   teaspoon coriander
1   tablespoon paprika
2   tablespoons brown sugar
1   teaspoon chili powder
1/4   teaspoon ground cloves
1/2   teaspoon onion powder
1/2   teaspoon garlic powder
1   teaspoon salt
1   teaspoon pepper

Braised Pork Belly

2   pounds pork belly
1/4   cup vegetable oil

Stock

1/2   onion, diced
2   celery ribs, diced
1   carrot, diced
1/4   cup Worcestershire sauce
2   cups orange juice
1/4   cup lemon juice
4   cups chicken stock or broth

Cilantro Foam

1   cup water
1   cup cilantro
1   package unflavored powdered gelatin

Tostones

2   cups vegetable oil
2   plantains, cut into coins
Salt to taste

For the pickled onions, boil the onions for 1 minute; drain. Combine the onions, vinegar and salt in a bowl. Add cold water just to cover.

For the dry rub, combine all of the ingredients in a bowl.

For the pork belly, coat the pork belly with the dry rub. Heat the oil over medium-high heat in a braising pan or large, deep skillet. Add the pork and sear on all sides. Remove from the skillet, reserving the pan drippings.

For the stock, reduce the heat to low and cook the onion, celery and carrot in the reserved pan drippings in the skillet for 20 minutes or until brown and caramelized, stirring occasionally. Add all of the remaining stock ingredients. Add the pork belly. Cover and cook for 2 hours until very tender. Remove the pork from the stock; discard the stock. Shred the pork. Let cool.

For the cilantro foam, combine the water, cilantro and gelatin in a bowl and let stand for 15 minutes. Use a hand blender to blend the mixture until it foams up.

For the tostones, heat the oil to 350 degrees in a deep skillet. Fry the plantains in the oil for 2 to 3 minutes. Remove from the oil and drain. Press down on the plantains to flatten them into patties. Sprinkle with salt.

To assemble, drain the onions. Top each tostone with braised pork, pickled onions and cilantro foam.

Blue Cheese Cheesecake

Makes 36 mini cheesecakes

Bread crumbs

36   ounces cream cheese,
      room temperature

28   ounces blue cheese,
      room temperature

14   eggs

3/4   cup heavy cream

4   tablespoons all-purpose flour

A few dashes of Tabasco sauce

Salt and black pepper to taste

Coat 36 muffin cups with nonstick cooking spray. Fill with bread crumbs, turning the cups to coat. Empty the excess crumbs. Refrigerate the prepared cups.

Beat the cream cheese in a standing mixer until completely smooth, scraping down the side of the bowl. Add the blue cheese and mix well, scraping down the side of the bowl. Add the eggs one at a time, beating well after each addition and scraping down the side of the bowl. Add the cream, flour, Tabasco, salt and pepper and mix well. Scrape the side of the bowl to ensure that the cheese and flour are well mixed.

Preheat the oven to 250 degrees. Scoop the cheesecake batter into the prepared muffin cups. Top with additional bread crumbs. Place the muffin cups in a larger baking pan. Add enough water to the baking pan to reach halfway up the tins. Bake for 20 minutes or until the filling is set and nearly firm in the center. Let cool at room temperature. Turn out onto a serving plate. Serve immediately or refrigerate. Reheat the cheesecakes in a microwave or conventional oven.

Watercress Salad with Walnut Vinaigrette

Makes 4 servings

Walnut Vinaigrette

3	ounces walnut oil
1	egg yolk
1	teaspoon chopped garlic
1	teaspoon chopped shallot
1	teaspoon chopped fresh thyme
3	ounces rice vinegar

Salad

2	bunches watercress, trimmed and cut into bite-size lengths
2	ounces blue cheese
16	Belgian endive leaves
2	blood oranges, sectioned

For the vinaigrette, beat the walnut oil into the egg yolk in a bowl gradually until the mixture combines and emulsifies. Add the garlic, shallot and thyme. Add the vinegar slowly, beating constantly until blended.

For the salad, combine the watercress and blue cheese in a bowl with the vinaigrette, tossing to coat. Arrange on a serving plate. Surround with endive leaves. Arrange the orange sections in the endive leaves.

If you are concerned about using a raw egg yolk, use an egg yolk pasteurized in its shell, which is sold at some specialty food stores, or use an equivalent amount of pasteurized egg substitute.

Green Bean Salad with Sherry Vinaigrette

Makes 4 servings

Sherry Vinaigrette

1   tablespoon minced onion
1   teaspoon minced garlic
1/4 cup sherry vinegar
1/2 cup olive oil
1/2 teaspoon sugar
1   teaspoon salt
1/2 teaspoon pepper

Salad

1   pound green beans
1   red onion, thinly sliced
1   red bell pepper, thinly sliced

For the vinaigrette, combine the onion, garlic, vinegar, olive oil, sugar, salt and pepper in a large bowl and mix well.

For the salad, trim the green beans. Cook in boiling water in a saucepan for 1 to 2 minutes until the beans turn bright green. Drain and cover with cold water to stop the cooking process. Add the beans, onion and bell pepper to the vinaigrette and toss to coat. Chill until serving time.

Thomas Jefferson is credited with introducing olive oil to the United States after seeing its healthful benefits as well as its ability to enhance his beloved salads.

Asian-Style Chicken Salad   Makes 4 servings

Sweet Sesame Soy Dressing

1/4	cup red wine vinegar
1/2	cup vegetable oil
3	tablespoons soy sauce
1	tablespoon sesame oil
3	tablespoons sweet chili sauce
1	tablespoon sugar
1	teaspoon salt
1/2	teaspoon pepper

Salad

1	pound napa cabbage, shredded
6	ounces shiitake mushrooms, sliced
1	small red onion, sliced (about 1/2 cup)
2/3	cup shredded carrots
1	teaspoon white sesame seeds
1	teaspoon black sesame seeds
1/2	bunch cilantro, chopped
1/4	cup mandarin orange sections
4	fully cooked breaded chicken breasts, chopped

For the dressing, combine the vinegar, vegetable oil, soy sauce, sesame oil, chili sauce, sugar, salt and pepper in a mixing bowl and mix well.

For the salad, combine the cabbage, mushrooms, onion, carrots, sesame seeds, cilantro, orange sections and chicken in a large bowl. Add the dressing and toss to coat.

Shrimp Cobb Salad

Makes 4 servings

Avocado Ranch Dressing

1	avocado
1/2	cup sour cream
2	tablespoons buttermilk
1	teaspoon white vinegar
1/4	teaspoon chopped parsley
1/4	teaspoon chopped dill
1/8	teaspoon salt
1/8	teaspoon onion powder
1/8	teaspoon garlic powder

Salad

6	ounces field greens
4	ounces romaine, chopped
12	shrimp, poached
4	ounces crumbled blue cheese
8	slices bacon, cooked and crumbled
1	cup diced tomato
4	hard-cooked eggs, diced

For the dressing, mash the avocado in a bowl. Add the sour cream, buttermilk, vinegar, parsley, dill, salt, onion powder and garlic powder and mix well. Chill until ready to serve.

For the salad, combine the greens and lettuce in a bowl. Add the dressing and toss to coat. Divide the lettuce mixture among four salad bowls. Arrange the shrimp, blue cheese, bacon, tomato and eggs on the lettuce.

While in France, Ambassador Jefferson became
fond of French cheeses such as the blue cheese used in
a number of the recipes featured here.

Monticello and The University

This bronze life–size figure of Thomas Jefferson was sculpted by Richmond native Moses Ezekiel. It was cast in Rome. Erected in 1910, it bears the legend: "To perpetuate the teachings and examples of the founders of the republic, this monument to Thomas Jefferson was presented to the people."

Aerial view of Monticello Vegetable Garden, Vineyard, and South Orchard © Thomas Jefferson Foundation at Monticello. photograph by Leonard Phillip

The University still profits from Jefferson's original garden plans, from the spring dogwood and redbud to the autumn colors and the winter presence of hollies and hemlocks. Fruit trees were a resource for the nearby University's first dining halls as well. At Monticello, extensive gardens featured 330 varieties and 89 species of vegetables and herbs in addition to 170 varieties of fruits. While both the kitchen at Monticello and the White House benefitted from blending European, Mediterranean, and Native American influences, Jefferson declared that vegetables constituted his principle dish. These influences and Jefferson's preferences are featured in these recipes for soups and side dishes.

The University of Virginia officially offers full and equal enrollment to graduate women.

1970

To commemorate the anniversary of America's independence, Britain's Queen Elizabeth II strolls the University of Virginia lawn and lunches in the Dome Room of the Rotunda, one of five American sites she visits publicly.

1976

Renovated as closely as possible according to plans from the 1800s, a now three-story Rotunda opens on the founder's birthday, April 13, 1976.

1976

"*I rank Botany with the most valuable sciences . . . its subjects as . . . delicious varieties for our tables, refreshments from our orchards, the adornments of our flower borders, shade and perfume of our groves . . .*"

—Thomas Jefferson, 1814

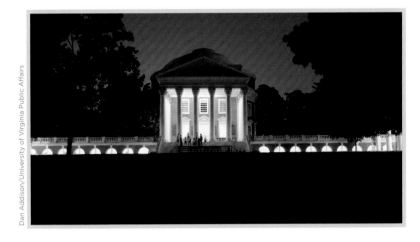

Dan Addison/University of Virginia Public Affairs

Monticello and the University of Virginia are named World Heritage Sites on UNESCO's prestigious World Heritage list, which includes the Taj Mahal, Versailles, and the Great Wall of China; UVA is the first collegiate campus worldwide to be awarded the designation.

The University of Virginia purchases Boar's Head property.

1987

1989

The University of Virginia

View of the Lawn

The Garden Book of Thomas Jefferson is now in the possession of the Massachusetts Historical Society, Boston, Massachusetts.

Eighteenth-century flowers found in the Pavilion Gardens today include:

HERBACEOUS FLOWERS

Aquilegia vulgaris (Columbine)
Campanula medium (Bellflower)
Celosia cristata (Cockscomb)
Consolida orientalis (Larkspur)
Convallaria majalis (Lily-of-the-valley)
Dianthus chinensis (Pinks)
Gomphrena globosa (Globe amaranth)
Heliotrope arborescens (Heliotrope)
Iris persica (Persian iris)
Jeffersonia diphylla (Twinleaf)
Lobelia cardinalis (Cardinal flower)
Mertensia virginica (Virginia bluebells)
Nigella sativa (Love-in-the-mist)
Papaver rhoeas (Corn poppy)
Tagetes patula (French marigold)

SHRUBS AND VINES

Callicarpa americana (Beauty-berry)
Calycanthus floridus (Sweet shrub)
Clethra alnifolia (Sweet pepper bush)
Hibiscus syriacus (Rose of Sharon)
Ilex opaca (American holly)
Kalmia latifolia (Mountain laurel)
Philadelphus coronarius (Mock orange)
Rhododendron maximum (Rosebay rhododendron)
Symphoricarpus albus (Snowberry)
Syringa persica (Persian lilac)
Viburnum trilobum (Bush cranberry)
Vitex agnus-castus (Chaste tree)
Wisteria frutescens (Wisteria)

Pavilion V garden

Pavilion VIII garden

Pavilion I garden
Tulips were wildly popular, including parrot and striped varieties.

Following are a few of the trees that Jefferson once grew and that now flourish in the Pavilion Gardens:

Albizia julibrissin (Mimosa)
Catalpa bignoiniodes (Southern catalpa)
Chionanthus virginicus (Fringe tree)
Gleditsia triacanthos (Honeylocust)
Halesia carolina (Silverbell)
Juglans nigra (Black walnut)
Koelreuteria paniculata (Goldenrain tree)
Liquidambar styraciflua (American sweetgum)
Liriodendron tulipifera (Tulip tree)
Magnolia virginiana (Sweetbay magnolia)
Magnolia grandiflora (Southern magnolia)
Malus "Albemarle Pippin" (Apple)
Morus rubra (Red mulberry)
Robinia pseudoacacia (Black locust)

Pavilion III garden

Jefferson grew 330 vegetable varieties in Monticello's 1,000-foot-long garden terrace.

Aerial view of Monticello Vegetable Garden, Vineyard, and South Orchard
© Thomas Jefferson Foundation at Monticello, photograph by Leonard Phill p

The main part of Jefferson's two-acre garden is divided into twenty-four "squares," or growing plots. In 1812 the squares were arranged according to which part of the plant was being harvested, whether "fruits" (tomatoes, beans), "roots" (beets, carrots), or "leaves" (lettuce, cabbage).

Between 1769 and 1814 Jefferson planted as many as 1,031 fruit trees in his South Orchard.

Sweet Potato Bisque with Raspberry Coulis

Makes 12 servings

1	yellow onion, roughly chopped	2	teaspoons allspice
1	celery rib, roughly chopped	2	teaspoons cinnamon
3	carrots, peeled and roughly chopped	1	cup honey
1/4	cup vegetable oil	1	cup brown sugar
5	pounds sweet potatoes, peeled and cubed	1/2	gallon (8 cups) milk

Raspberry Coulis (recipe below)

Micro greens or sliced green onions

Sauté the onion, celery and carrots in the oil in a stockpot until tender. Add the sweet potatoes and water to cover. Add the spices, honey and brown sugar. Bring to a boil. Reduce the heat to low and simmer until the sweet potatoes are very soft; drain, reserving the cooking liquid. Purée the vegetables in batches in a blender or food processor. Add the cooking liquid as needed for a manageable consistency. (The soup maybe prepared up to this point and refrigerated until ready to use.) Add the milk and heat through. To serve, top each bowl of bisque with raspberry coulis and micro greens.

Raspberry Coulis

1	pint raspberries	1	tablespoon sugar
1/4	cup water	1/4	teaspoon vanilla extract
	Juice of 1 lemon	1/8	teaspoon cayenne pepper

Purée all the ingredients in a blender. Strain to remove the seeds.

Crab Risotto

Makes 10 servings

1	medium onion, diced	5	cups chicken broth, heated
1	celery rib, diced	1	cup heavy cream
4	garlic cloves, minced	3/4	cup grated Parmesan cheese
1/4	cup extra-virgin olive oil	2	pounds crab meat
2 1/2	cups arborio rice		Kosher salt and white pepper
3/4	cup white wine		to taste

Sauté the onion, celery and garlic in the olive oil in a large saucepan until tender. Add the rice and stir to coat. Do not allow the rice to brown. Add the wine and cook over medium heat, stirring constantly, until the liquid is evaporated. Add sufficient broth to just cover the rice. Cook until the liquid is absorbed, stirring constantly. Add more broth a little at a time, cooking and stirring until the rice is tender but still firm in the center. Do not allow the rice to boil.

Add the heavy cream and cheese to the risotto and mix gently. Add the crab meat, reserving about 1/4 cup for garnish. Ladle the risotto into soup bowls. Top each serving with a heaping teaspoon of crab meat.

Smuggling the grain out of Italy,
Jefferson introduced upland rice (a variety he
considered superior) to Virginia.

Sweet Potato Risotto

Makes 6 servings

1	pound arborio rice	1/4	cup heavy cream
1/4	cup minced shallots	1/4	cup butter
2	tablespoons olive oil	1	cup grated Parmesan cheese
4	cups chicken stock, heated	Salt and white pepper to taste	
4	medium sweet potatoes, diced small		

Sauté the rice and shallots in olive oil in a large saucepan until translucent. Add the chicken stock 1/2 cup at a time, and cook, stirring, until most of the liquid is absorbed. Repeat until 3 cups of the stock are used.

Add the sweet potatoes and cream. Add 1/2 cup of the remaining stock and cook, stirring, until most of it is absorbed. Test the sweet potatoes and rice; if they are tender, the risotto is finished. If they are still firm, add the remaining 1/2 cup of stock and cook until it is absorbed, stirring constantly.

Fold in the butter and cheese. Season with salt and pepper.

*Sweet potatoes were grown at
Monticello, where the cooks created a
number of ways to serve them.*

Vegetarian Cannelloni

Makes 4 servings

1 cup ricotta cheese	1/4 cup kalamata olives
1/4 cup shredded mozzarella cheese	4 tablespoons olive oil
	Salt and pepper to taste
1/4 cup grated Parmesan cheese	4 (6-inch) frozen pasta sheets, thawed
1 cup fresh spinach	Your favorite tomato basil cream
1 bell pepper, diced	Your favorite marinara sauce
1/2 small zucchini, diced	Fresh or dried basil to taste
1/2 small yellow squash, diced	

Preheat the oven to 350 degrees. Combine the ricotta, mozzarella and Parmesan in a bowl and mix well. Sauté the spinach, bell pepper, zucchini, squash and olives in the olive oil in a skillet until tender. Let cool. Fold into the ricotta mixture.

Place a large spoonful of the ricotta mixture on each pasta sheet. Roll to enclose the filling.

Arrange the rolls on a baking sheet. Combine the tomato basil cream, marinara sauce and basil in a bowl and mix well. Pour the desired amount over the rolls. Bake for 20 minutes.

Capellini Flan

Makes 4 servings

2   cups cooked capellini or
     angel hair pasta

1/2 cup shredded
     Parmesan cheese

1   tablespoon chopped chives
     or parsley

2   tablespoons extra-virgin
     olive oil

Kosher salt and pepper to taste

1   cup heavy cream

3   large eggs

Preheat the oven to 350 degrees. Combine the pasta, cheese, chives and olive oil in a
bowl. Add salt and pepper and mix well.

Coat four 4-ounce aluminum baking cups with nonstick cooking spray. Fill the cups to
the top with the pasta mixture. Arrange the cups on a baking sheet.

Whisk together the cream and eggs in a bowl. Fill the cups with the mixture.

Place the cups in the oven. Turn the heat to 300 degrees and bake for 25 minutes or
until a wooden pick inserted in the center comes out clean. Bake 5 minutes longer
if needed.

*An imported version of macaroni
and cheese was served at both Monticello
and the Jefferson White House.*

Capellini with Shrimp, Crab, Jalapeño, Lime, Tomato and Cilantro

Makes 4 servings

1	tablespoon chopped garlic		Juice of 2 limes
1	jalapeño chile, minced	1/8	teaspoon salt
3	tablespoons vegetable oil	1/8	teaspoon pepper to taste
12	jumbo shrimp	3	tablespoons chopped cilantro
8	ounces jumbo lump crab meat	3	tablespoons butter
1	cup diced tomato	1	pound hot cooked capellini

Sauté the garlic and jalapeño in the oil in a sauté pan. Add the shrimp, crab and tomato and cook over high heat until the shrimp are opaque. Add the lime juice, salt, pepper and cilantro. Stir in the butter.

Divide the pasta among four bowls. Top with the seafood mixture.

After discovering the pleasures of pasta
while in Europe, Thomas Jefferson designed a
pasta-making machine to bring back home.

Grilled Beets and Vidalia Onion in Rosemary Vinegar

Make 4 servings

1/3	cup balsamic vinegar	1	Vidalia onion, sliced
2	tablespoons olive oil	3	medium beets, peeled
1	tablespoon chopped		and sliced
	fresh rosemary		Salt and pepper to taste
2	garlic cloves, minced		

Combine the vinegar, olive oil, rosemary and garlic in a bowl and mix well. Add the onion and beets and stir to coat. Let stand for at least 20 minutes.

Heat a grill to high heat. Wrap the beets and onion in aluminum foil and seal tightly. Place the packet on the grill. Cook for 20 to 25 minutes until the beets are tender. Serve as a side dish with grilled fish or poultry.

Candied Leeks

Makes 4 servings

1	leek, white part only, juliennéd	1/4	cup simple syrup

Preheat the oven to 225 degrees. Boil the leeks briefly in salted water. Drain and cool slightly. Pat dry. Combine the leeks and simple syrup and toss to coat. Spread the leeks over a baking pan. Bake until caramelized.

Braised Red Cabbage

Makes 10 servings

1/4	onion, diced	1/4	cup red wine
2	tablespoons vegetable oil	1/4	cup red wine vinegar
1 1/2	pounds red cabbage, shredded	1	tablespoon brown sugar
1	tablespoon butter	1	cup vegetable stock

Sauté the onion in the oil in a saucepan. Add the cabbage, butter, wine, vinegar, brown sugar and stock. Cover and cook over low heat until the cabbage is tender. Check occasionally and add more liquid if needed.

Asian Slaw

Makes about 2 cups

2	tablespoons chopped fresh cilantro	1	teaspoon salt
2	tablespoons rice wine vinegar	1/2	teaspoon pepper
2	tablespoons sriracha chile paste	1/4	head cabbage, julienned
1/2	cup mayonnaise	2	carrots, shredded
		1/3	red bell pepper, julienned
		1	green onion, finely chopped

Combine the cilantro, vinegar, chile paste, mayonnaise, salt and pepper in a medium bowl and mix well. Add the cabbage, carrots, bell pepper and onion and mix to coat.

Boar's Head

A state-of-the-art sports club, award-winning tennis, championship golf, and a luxurious spa await visitors of Boar's Head. The first-class facilities and ambiance at the Sports Club allow members and guests the opportunity to enjoy a healthy lifestyle in a family-friendly environment. With twenty-six indoor and outdoor tennis courts, a squash facility housing eight international singles courts, one championship court, two North American doubles courts, fifty weekly exercise classes, a rock wall, outdoor aquatics facilities, children's programs, and a fitness room overlooking one of the most beautiful vistas in Charlottesville, there is something for everyone at the Sports Club.

Boar's Head Sports Club is constructed.

Felicia Warburg Rogan, wife of Boar's Head founder, opens Oakencroft Vineyard and Winery on their Albemarle cattle farm.

1974

1983

"*The original fieldstones, heartwood pine beams, planking, and massive grist stones are now prominently featured throughout the main inn.*"

—THE BOAR'S HEAD INN BROCHURE, C. 1964

John Rogan, founder of Boar's Head, dies at age 71.

Boar's Head property is acquired by the University of Virginia.

1988

1989

The Sports Club, Spa, and Pavilion

In addition, the 33,000 square foot McArthur Squash Center opened in 2013, greatly expanding the University of Virginia's squash program. All facilities are available to Boar's Head guests and members. Just as our sports club has something for every taste, the following main dishes will tempt those whose tastes run from fine dining to those whose preference is an all-American hamburger.

The Spa at Boar's Head is built.

Boyd Tinsley Courts are constructed at Boar's Head Sports Club

Felicia Rogan closes the winery and sells Oakencroft Farm.

2000

2006

2008

The parcel of land on which the Boar's Head is situated was previously the Ednam Estate.

The Meeting Pavilion (Boar's Head new conference center) opens, Glave Holmes Architects

Boar's Head

2008

2011

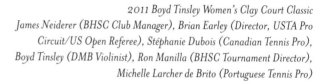

2011 Boyd Tinsley Women's Clay Court Classic
James Neiderer (BHSC Club Manager), Brian Earley (Director, USTA Pro
Circuit/US Open Referee), Stéphanie Dubois (Canadian Tennis Pro),
Boyd Tinsley (DMB Violinist), Ron Manilla (BHSC Tournament Director),
Michelle Larcher de Brito (Portuguese Tennis Pro)

Arch detail

Boar's Head fountain

Relaxing at the Spa

The Future of Boar's Head

Rest your mind and let the world melt away when you treat yourself to a day at The Spa at Boar's Head. Feel your cares slipping away as our staff of talented therapists soothes your body and soul in a tranquil environment. Indulge in a rejuvenating facial and allow us to soothe your sore muscles and beautify your hands and feet. Afterward, relax on the balcony or terrace of your guest room while enjoying the picturesque surroundings of the Piedmont countryside, or cozy up to the fireplace in your guest suite.

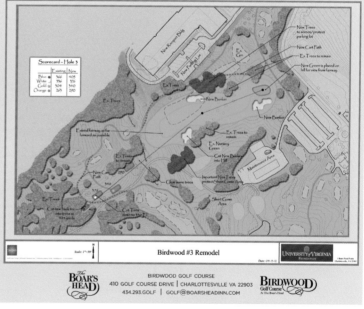

Renovations start on property enhancement projects such as purchasing new fitness equipment, resurfacing several indoor tennis courts, re-roofing buildings, painting, upgrading the walkways, and much more.

Renovations began on hole number #3 at Birdwood. The new hole has a slight dog-leg to the right, with a reshaped fairway, a new green, and a new cart path.

McArthur Squash Center under construction.

2011

2012

*"You savor the continuity of history. . .
The land you stroll across was this
section's first clearing in th wilderness,
a lordly plantation before the Revolution.*

—THE BOAR'S HEAD INN BROCHURE, C. 1964

Guest rooms renovations
are completed.

The University of Virginia's
McArthur Squash Center opens.

2012   2013

University of Virginia Foundation Headquarters

Grilled Thyme- and- Garlic-Marinated Veal Chop

Makes 4 to 6 servings

2   sprigs of fresh thyme

6   tablespoons olive oil

1   garlic clove, minced

1   teaspoon salt

1/2   teaspoon pepper

4   veal chops

Braised Red Cabbage (page 99)

Mustard Spaetzle (page 87)

Combine the thyme, olive oil, garlic, salt and pepper in a bowl and mix well. Add the veal chops and turn to coat. Let marinate for 1 hour. Preheat the grill. Grill the chops over medium heat to the desired doneness. Serve with Braised Red Cabbage and Mustard Spaetzle.

*Although Jefferson preferred a mostly
vegetarian diet, a variety of meats were served at
each formal White House dinner.*

Pineland Farms Tenderloin of Beef "Chesapeake Style"

Makes 4 servings

Lemon Hollandaise Sauce

2	cups butter
6	egg yolks
1	teaspoon white vinegar
3	tablespoons white wine
1	tablespoon lemon juice
1/8	teaspoon salt
1/8	teaspoon white pepper
3	dashes of hot sauce

Olive Oil-Poached Tomatoes

1	pound heirloom tomatoes, coarsely chopped
1/8	teaspoon salt
	Pepper to taste
1	tablespoon sugar
4	garlic cloves, minced
5	sprigs fresh thyme
2	cups (about) olive oil

Jumbo Lump Crab-Topped Filets

4	(6-ounce) beef filets
	Salt and pepper to taste
8	ounces jumbo lump crab meat
2	tablespoons melted butter
2	ounces panko
1	teaspoon chopped parsley
1	teaspoon chopped chives
12	green asparagus spears, cooked
8	white asparagus spears, cooked
2	ounces beef demi-glace

For the hollandaise sauce, melt the butter in a saucepan until it foams. Ladle off the clear butter, discarding the solids at the bottom of the pan. Combine the clarified butter with the egg yolks, wine, vinegar, lemon juice and hot sauce in a stainless steel bowl set over a pan of simmering water. Whisk until the mixture thickens.

For the tomatoes, preheat the oven to 175 degrees. Arrange the tomatoes in one layer in a baking dish. Season with the salt and pepper. Sprinkle with the sugar, garlic and thyme. Add enough olive oil to almost cover tomatoes. Bake for 1 to 1½ hours or until tender.

For the filets, preheat the oven to 350 degrees. Season the filets with salt and pepper. Heat a sauté pan over medium-high heat and sear the filets. Combine the crab, butter, panko, parsley and chives in a small bowl. Divide the mixture into four portions. Pat one portion onto each filet. Bake until the filets reach the desired doneness.

To serve, divide the asparagus among four plates. Place a filet next to the asparagus. Spoon Lemon Hollandaise over both. Garnish with 8 ounces of the Olive Oil-Poached Tomatoes. Drizzle the demi-glace around the filet.

Pistachio-Crusted Rack of Lamb

Makes 2 servings

1/2	cup olive oil	1	tablespoon minced garlic
1	sprig of fresh rosemary, minced	1	(8-bone) rack of lamb, frenched
1	tablespoon crushed juniper berries	1/2	cup vegetable oil
1	tablespoon kosher salt	2	tablespoons Dijon mustard
1	tablespoon crushed black peppercorns	1	cup pistachios, crushed

Combine the first six ingredients in a large bowl. Add the lamb and marinate in the refrigerator for at least 4 hours. Remove the lamb from the marinade; discard the marinade.

Preheat the oven to 350 degrees. Heat the vegetable oil in a large, heavy sauté pan over medium-high heat. Sear the lamb all over. Remove from the heat and let cool to handling temperature. Cover the exposed bones with aluminum foil. Spread the mustard over the fat side of the lamb. Cover with crushed pistachios, pressing them into the mustard.

Arrange the lamb crust side up in a roasting pan. Roast for 45 minutes or until the lamb registers 140 degrees on a meat thermometer. Cover the crust with foil if needed to prevent it from overbrowning. Remove the lamb from the oven and let stand 5 minutes. Hold bones in a vertical position and cut down through the meat.

Boar's Head Ultimate Burger

Makes 4 servings

4	(8-ounce) ground sirloin patties	4	slices tomato
4	slices aged Cheddar cheese	4	very thin slices red onion
8	slices applewood-smoked bacon, crisp-cooked	2	ounces arugula, or 4 romaine leaves
4	artisan kaiser rolls or buns		Sweet Potato Fries (recipe below)

Prepare a fire in a grill and grill the burgers to the desired doneness. Top with cheese and bacon. Place the burgers on the buns and top with the tomato, onion and arugula. Serve with Sweet Potato Fries and your favorite condiments.

Sweet Potato Fries

	Vegetable oil for frying	1	cup cornstarch
4	sweet potatoes, cut into sticks	1	teaspoon salt

Fill a fryer with oil and heat according to the manufacturer's directions. Cover the cut sweet potatoes with cold water. Drain and pat dry. Combine with the cornstarch, tossing to coat. Discard the excess cornstarch. Fry the sweet potatoes in the oil, in batches if necessary, until golden brown. Drain well. Season with the salt.

The recipe for "pommes frites" brought back from France inspired this version.

Chicken with Sun-Dried Tomatoes and Asparagus

Makes 4 servings

1	teaspoon dried basil	4	boneless skinless
1	teaspoon dried oregano		chicken breasts
2	cups fresh bread crumbs	20	asparagus spears, blanched
	or panko	1	cup sun-dried
1/2	cup olive oil		tomatoes, sliced
Salt and pepper to taste		1	cup olive oil

Preheat the oven to 350 degrees. Combine the basil, oregano, bread crumbs, 1/2 cup olive oil, salt and pepper in a bowl and mix well.

Pound the chicken to an even thickness. Season with salt and pepper. Arrange 5 asparagus spears, 1/4 cup of the tomatoes and some of the bread crumb mixture on the short end of each piece of chicken. Roll to enclose the filling. Secure with a wooden pick if needed. Arrange seam side down on a parchment-covered baking sheet. Drizzle with 1 cup olive oil.

Bake for 15 to 20 minutes until the filling is hot and the chicken is cooked through.

Chicken Roulade

Makes 6 servings

2	tablespoons chopped garlic	6	ounces spinach leaves
1	medium shallot, chopped	5	ounces boursin cheese
2	tablespoons olive oil	Salt and pepper to taste	
1/4	cup white wine	6	(6-ounce) boneless skinless
12	ounces mixed shiitake, portobello and oyster mushrooms, sliced		chicken breasts

Sauté the garlic and shallots in the olive oil in a sauté pan until tender. Add the wine, mushrooms and spinach and cook until the spinach wilts. Remove from the heat and add the cheese. Stir to blend. Season with salt and pepper. Let stand to cool.

Preheat the oven to 350 degrees. Cut each chicken breast horizontally without cutting through so it may be opened like a book. Pound to an even thickness with a meat mallet. Place a spoonful of the spinach mixture at one end of the meat. Roll to enclose the filling.

Place the roulades seam side down on a baking sheet. Bake for 25 minutes or until the internal temperature is 165 degrees. Cut each roulade into three pieces to serve.

Herb-Roasted Chicken

Makes 4 servings

4	chicken breasts	2	tablespoons vegetable oil
Zest of 1 lemon		1	tablespoon butter
1	teaspoon rosemary, chopped	Goat Cheese–Laced Stone-	
1	teaspoon fresh thyme, chopped		Ground Grits (page 87)
		a.m. FOG Mushroom Ragout	
1/8	teaspoon salt		(recipe follows)
1/8	teaspoon pepper		

Preheat the oven to 350 degrees. Season the chicken with the lemon zest, rosemary, thyme, salt and pepper. Sear the chicken in the oil in a sauté pan with an ovenproof handle. Add the butter to the pan and place the pan in the oven. Cook until the chicken is 165 degrees. Remove from the oven. Baste the chicken with the pan drippings. Slice the chicken and serve over the cheese grits. Top with a.m. FOG Mushroom Ragout and garnish with fresh herb salad.

a.m. FOG Mushroom Ragout

2	tablespoons olive oil	1/4	cup white wine
1	tablespoon butter	1/4	cup demi-glace
1/4	cup minced shallots	1/8	teaspoon pepper
1	pound a.m. FOG mushrooms	1/8	teaspoon salt

Heat the olive oil and butter in a sauté pan over medium-high heat. Sauté the shallots briefly, then add the mushrooms and sauté until cooked through. Add the wine and cook, scraping up any brown bits. Cook until the mixture is reduced slightly. Add the demi-glace, salt and pepper.

Crab-Crusted Sea Bass with Smoked Tomato and Red Pepper Compote

Make 4 servings

4	(6-ounce) sea bass fillets	2	tablespoons melted butter
Salt and pepper to taste		1/4	cup panko
Vegetable oil		1	teaspoon chopped parsley
3	tablespoons stone-ground mustard	1	teaspoon chopped chives
1	tablespoon honey		Smoked Tomato and Red Pepper Compote (page 86)
8	ounces jumbo lump crab meat		Red and Yellow Pepper Salad (page 86)

Preheat the oven to 350 degrees. Season the fish with salt and pepper. Heat a small amount of oil in a large skillet with an ovenproof handle. Sear the fish on both sides. Brush with a mixture of the mustard and honey. Combine the crab meat, butter, panko, parsley and chives in a bowl. Top each fillet evenly with the crab mixture.

Bake until fish is cooked through and topping is hot. Serve with Smoked Tomato and Red Pepper Compote and Red and Yellow Pepper Salad.

Pesto-Marinated Swordfish with Sauce Provençale

Makes 4 servings

Pesto

1¼ cups basil leaves
6 tablespoons olive oil
2 tablespoons grated Parmesan cheese
1 teaspoon chopped garlic
1 tablespoon pine nuts, toasted

Swordfish

4 swordfish steaks
Olive oil

Sauce Provençale

2 teaspoons chopped garlic
1 teaspoon chopped shallot
Olive oil for sautéing
¼ cup chardonnay
1 teaspoon oregano
4 roma tomatoes, peeled, seeded and chopped
1 teaspoon chiffonade-cut basil
2 tablespoons butter
Salt and white pepper to taste

For the pesto, combine the basil, olive oil, cheese, garlic and pine nuts in a blender. Process until the mixture forms a paste.

For the swordfish, spread the pesto on the fish. Drizzle lightly with olive oil. Refrigerate for at least 8 hours. Grill the swordfish to desired doneness.

For the sauce, sauté the garlic and shallot in the olive oil in a saucepan. Add the wine and oregano and cook until reduced by three-fourths. Add the tomato and basil and heat through. Remove from the heat; add the butter and mix well. Season with salt and white pepper. Spoon over the swordfish to serve.

New Traditions

Entrance to Boar's Head

Traditions can begin with a first visit and be passed down with each return. Some traditions, like the annual Turkey Trot and afternoon tea, have existed for many years; some traditions, like high tea and carriage rides, have been reinstated; while others, like our annual Tree Lighting, are only a few years old. Share with us the fun of moving from one tradition to another while creating your own traditions. For this is the essence of Boar's Head—a profusion of moments that bond families firmly and promote conversations that last a lifetime. Please enjoy!

The Old Mill Room, Boar's Head

*If we want to understand
ourselves, we would do well
to take a searching look at
our landscapes.*

—Pierce F. Lewis, American Geographer, 1979

Boar's Head fountain

Boar's Head

Fruit Smoothie — Three Ways

Makes 1 serving

1 cup vanilla yogurt	1/2 cup passion fruit, raspberry
1/2 cup milk	or kiwi purée
6 tablespoons sugar	Passion fruit seeds, raspberries
1 teaspoon vanilla extract	or kiwi slices for garnish

Combine the yogurt, milk, sugar, vanilla and fruit purée of your choice in a blender. Process until well blended. Pour into a tall glass. Garnish with fresh fruit.

Berries with Champagne Sabayon

Makes 4 servings

Berries

1 pint strawberries, hulled

1 pint blueberries

1 pint blackberries

Sabayon

3 ounces sugar

3 ounces Champagne

3 egg yolks

For the berries, wash and rinse dry. Cut the strawberries into quarters.

For the sabayon, combine the sugar, Champagne and egg yolks in a medium metal bowl. Whisk to blend. Set the bowl over, not in, a pan of simmering water. Heat, whisking often, for 5 to 10 minutes until the mixture is thick and forms a ribbon when drizzled from a spoon.

Divide the berries among 6 serving dishes or sundae glasses. Top with the sabayon.

While in France, Ambassador Jefferson developed
a taste for fine French wines. He later served Champagne
at nearly every White House dinner.

Boar's Head
Good Morning Waffles

Makes 6 waffles

2	eggs	1/4	teaspoon salt
2	cups all-purpose flour	1/2	teaspoon vanilla extract
1 3/4	cups milk		Maple syrup
1/2	cup vegetable oil		Confectioners' sugar
1	tablespoon sugar		Whipped butter
1	tablespoon baking powder		Fresh berries

Preheat a waffle iron. Whisk the eggs in a mixing bowl until fluffy. Add the flour, milk, oil, sugar, baking powder, salt and vanilla and mix until smooth and well blended.

Spray the hot waffle iron with nonstick cooking spray. Pour batter onto the iron and cook until golden brown according to the manufacturer's directions. Serve hot waffles with a choice of maple syrup, confectioners' sugar, whipped butter and/or fresh berries.

After discovering waffles in Amsterdam,
Jefferson bought a waffle iron to bring home so he
could share the breakfast treat with America.

Crab Cakes Benedict

Makes 4 servings

Crab Cakes

3	tablespoons mayonnaise
1	egg, beaten
2	tablespoons diced red bell pepper
2	tablespoons diced yellow bell pepper
1/4	teaspoon hot red pepper sauce
1/2	teaspoon Old Bay seasoning
1	pound lump crab meat
1/4	cup bread crumbs
1	tablespoon melted butter

Vegetable oil for frying
Butter for frying

Sautéed Spinach

1/4	onion, diced
1	tablespoon vegetable oil
1	pound fresh spinach

Salt and pepper to taste

Hollandaise Sauce

2	cups (1 pound) butter
6	egg yolks
3	tablespoons white wine
1	teaspoon white vinegar
1	tablespoon lemon juice
3	dashes of hot red pepper sauce
1/8	teaspoon salt
1/8	teaspoon white pepper

Assembly

4	English muffins, split and toasted
8	slices tomato
8	poached eggs

For the crab cakes, combine the mayonnaise, egg, bell peppers, hot sauce and Old Bay in a bowl and mix well. Add the crab meat, bread crumbs and butter and mix well. Form the mixture into 8 patties. Heat a little vegetable oil and butter in a sauté pan. Cook the crab cakes until golden brown on both sides. Keep warm.

For the spinach, sauté the onion in the oil in a large sauté pan. Add the spinach and cook until the spinach wilts, tossing frequently. Season with salt and pepper.

For the hollandaise sauce, heat the butter in a saucepan until it foams. Ladle off the clear butter, leaving the solids that sink to the bottom. Combine the egg yolks, wine, vinegar, lemon juice and hot sauce in a heatproof bowl. Set the bowl over, not in, a pan of simmering water. Heat the mixture for 3 to 5 minutes until it thickens, whisking constantly.

Remove the bowl and whisk in the clarified butter. Add the salt and white pepper.

To assemble, arrange one muffin on each serving plate. Top each muffin half with a tomato slice, some sautéed spinach, a crab cake and a poached egg. Top with hollandaise sauce and serve immediately.

140

'Twas the season of Christmas and all through the house...

Nutcrackers guard the chimney with care.

In hopes that St. Nicholas soon would be there.

Visions of sugarplums decorate the Old Mill Room.

A Merry Cavalier Christmas

Yes, Virginia, there is a Santa Claus.

The annual Tree Lighting

To the top of the porch, to the top of the wall...Merry Christmas to all!

Chocolate Decadence

Makes 12 servings

1	pound (2 cups) butter	3/4	cup cocoa powder
1	pound semisweet chocolate	3	ounces coffee-flavored
1	pound (2 cups) sugar		liqueur
12	eggs		

Preheat the oven to 350 degrees Grease and flour a 9×13-inch baking pan.

Melt the chocolate with the butter and sugar in a microwave-safe bowl, or in the top of a double boiler. Remove from the heat. Beat in the eggs until thoroughly combined. Stir in the cocoa powder. Add the liqueur and mix well. Spoon the batter into the prepared pan. Bake for 20 minutes or until just set but not firm. Serve warm.

"The superiority of chocolate, both for health and nourishment, will soon give it the same preference over tea and coffee in America which it has in Spain."
—*Thomas Jefferson*

Crème Brûlée

Makes 8 servings

6	egg yolks	1	vanilla bean, split
1/2	cup sugar		lengthwise
2	cups heavy cream		Additional sugar

Preheat the oven to 350 degrees.

Beat the egg yolks and sugar in a bowl until well blended.

Heat the cream and vanilla bean in a saucepan to the scalding point. Pour gradually into the egg mixture, stirring constantly. Divide the mixture among 8 ovenproof custard cups.

Place the cups in a large baking dish and put the dish on the oven rack. Add enough water to the baking dish to reach halfway up the cups. Bake for 25 minutes or until the custard is set. Refrigerate until cool.

To serve, sprinkle a little sugar on each custard. Use a kitchen torch to brown the sugar until it is caramelized.

Chocolate Cheesecake

Makes 16 servings.

Crust

2	cups finely ground Oreo cookie crumbs
1/2	cup butter, melted

Ganache

1	cup heavy cream
8	ounces 65% chocolate

Filling

56	ounces cream cheese
3	cups sugar
1	cup cocoa powder
1	cup heavy cream
6	egg yolks
1/4	teaspoon vanilla extract
8	eggs

For the crust, grease the bottom and sides of a large sheet pan and line with baking parchment. Combine the cookie crumbs and butter in a bowl and stir until the mixture holds together. Pat over the bottom of the prepared pan.

For the ganache, bring the cream to a boil in a saucepan over medium heat, stirring frequently. Pour over the chocolate in a bowl and whisk until blended.

For the filling, beat the cream cheese in a large bowl at medium speed for 2 to 10 minutes or until softened. Reduce the mixer speed and beat for 2 minutes. Combine the sugar and cocoa powder in a bowl and mix well. Add to the cream cheese and beat on low just until blended, scraping the bottom and side of the bowl occasionally. Beat in the cream, egg yolks and vanilla slowly. Add the eggs one at a time, beating well after each addition. Add the ganache and beat until blended. Pour over the crust. Bake at 300 degrees for 40 to 55 minutes or until set.

Gold Standard Bread Pudding

Makes 6 to 8 servings

5	egg yolks
2	cups heavy cream
1/3	cup sugar
1/2	ounce vanilla syrup
1	loaf bread

Preheat the oven to 350 degrees. Combine the egg yolks, cream, sugar and vanilla syrup in a bowl and mix well. Cut the bread into small pieces. Combine with the egg mixture, allowing the bread to absorb it. Spoon the mixture into a greased 9×13-inch baking pan. Bake for 1 hour or until golden brown.

Variations

For mango bread pudding, add 1 cup diced fresh or frozen mangoes.

For peach bread pudding, add 1 cup diced fresh or frozen peaches.

*Bread pudding was a favorite
Monticello dessert varied here with peaches,
Jefferson's favorite fruit.*

Bourbon Chocolate Pecan Pie

Makes 2 pies

Sugar Cookie Crust

3/4 cup sugar

13/4 cups (31/2 sticks) butter, softened

1 egg

1 tablespoon vanilla extract

2 cups bread flour

Pecan Filling

8 eggs

12/3 cups light brown sugar

1/2 cup light corn syrup

1/2 cup molasses

1 teaspoon salt

1 tablespoon vanilla extract

1/4 cup bourbon

6 tablespoons unsalted butter, melted

20 ounces pecans, toasted and chopped

3/4 cup chocolate chips

For the crust, preheat the oven to 350 degrees. Combine the sugar, butter egg and vanilla in a mixing bowl. Beat at low speed just until combined. Add the flour and mix just to combine. Cover and refrigerate for 30 minutes until firm enough to handle. Roll the dough on a floured surface to 1/4-inch thickness. Fit the dough into two greased and floured pie plates. Trim any overhanging dough. Bake for 20 minutes. Maintain the oven temperature

For the filling, beat the eggs with an electric mixer for 1 minute. Add the brown sugar, corn syrup, molasses, salt, vanilla and bourbon and mix well. Stir in the butter, pecans and chocolate. Pour the filling into the pie crusts. Bake for 35 minutes or until the filling is set, covering the edge of the edge of the crust with aluminum foil to prevent overbrowning if needed. Cool completely before serving.

Bavarian Cream with Vanilla Sponge Cake

Makes 8 servings

Vanilla Sponge Cake

2	pounds sugar
25	ounces cake flour
1	ounce baking powder
1/4	ounce salt
1	pound vegetable shortening
1 1/2	cups milk
2 1/4	cups eggs, beaten
1	teaspoon vanilla extract

Bavarian Cream

3	cups heavy whipping cream
1	ounce unflavored gelatin powder
1 1/4	cups cold water
4	cups milk
4	vanilla beans, split
12	egg yolks
10	ounces sugar

For the cake, whisk the first 4 ingredients in a bowl. Beat in the shortening on low speed until blended. Add milk, eggs and vanilla. Beat on low speed just until blended. Beat on medium speed for 3 minutes, then on medium-high speed for 5 minutes. Pour into a greased and floured 9×13-inch cake pan. Bake at 325 degrees for 20 minutes.

For the cream, whip the cream in a small bowl until soft peaks form; chill. Soften the gelatin in the cold water. Bring the milk and vanilla beans to a boil; set aside. Beat egg yolks and sugar in a bowl at medium speed until thick. Stir 1 cup hot milk gradually into the beaten eggs. Blend in the remaining milk gradually. Pour into the saucepan. Cook over low heat until thickened, stirring constantly. Whisk in the gelatin mixture. Strain into a bowl; place into a larger bowl filled with ice to cool. Fold in the whipped cream. Pour into molds and chill until firm.

To serve, unmold one Bavarian cream onto each portion of cake. Decorate and serve with fresh berries and Champagne Sabayon (page 137).

Index of Recipes

Additional Reading List

R. B. Bernstein
Thomas Jefferson

Thomas J. Craughwell
Thomas Jefferson's Crème Brûlée

William Hageman
"America's First Foodie,"
Chicago Tribune

Peter Hatch
*Thomas Jefferson's
Flower Garden at Monticello*
*"A Rich Spot of Earth": Thomas
Jefferson's Revolutionary
Garden at Monticello*

Marie Kimball
Thomas Jefferson's Cookbook

Historical Photo Credits

These images appear on pages 8–24.

A map of the most inhabited part of virginia containing the whole Province of Maryland with part of Pensilvania, New Jersey and North Carolina
Joshua Fry (1718–1754) and Peter Jefferson (1708–1757)
Thomas Jefferys (ca. 1719–1771), Engraver
Library of Virginia

University of Virginia
University of Virginia Visual History Collection. RG-30/1/10.011. Special Collections, University of Virginia, Charlottesville, VA

K. Edward Lay Papers, Accession #12817-a, Special Collections, University of Virginia, Charlottesville, VA

Holsinger Studio Collection, ca. 1890-1938, Accession #9862, Special Collections, University of Virginia, Charlottesville, VA

West Virginia: The Rand-McNally Vest pocket map of West Virginia, showing all counties, cities, towns, railways, lakes, rivers, etc. G3891.P3 1908. R2. Special Collections, University of Virginia, Charlottesville, VA

A new and historical map of Albemarle County, Virginia. G3883 .A3 1907 .M3. Special Collections, University of Virginia, Charlottesville, VA

Artist Jean Pierre Henri Louis Hore Browse Trist (1775-1804)
probably 1789/99
Yale University Art Gallery
Mabel Brady Garvan Collection

Jefferson's sketch of Monticello I or first house.
© Thomas Jefferson Foundation in Monticello

A new and historical map of Albemarle County, Virginia. G3883 .A3 1907 .M3. Special Collections, University of Virginia, Charlottesville, VA

Trustees' sales of most valuable farms!: Horses, oxen, cattle, hogs, sheep , farming implem'ts, household and kitchen furniture, &c., in Albemarle County.
:By virtue of a deed of trust executed on the 29th day of April 1875, by J. Woods Garth and wife,. Broadside 1875 .T78. Special Collections, University of Virginia, Charlottesville, VA

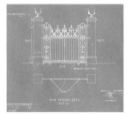

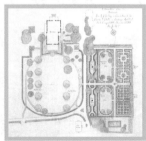

Historical Photo Credits

These images appear on pages 24–34.

© Thinkstock

Monticello, 1825, by Jane Braddick Peticolas
© Thomas Jefferson Foundation at Monticello, photograph by H. Andrew Johnson

Silhouette of Thomas Jefferson
Prints File. Special Collections.
University of Virginia, Charlottesville, VA

Rotunda and Pavilion I, from the south.
University of Virginia Visual History Collection. RG-30/1/10.011.
Special Collections, University of Virginia, Charlottesville, VA

© Thinkstock

© Thinkstock

© Thinkstock

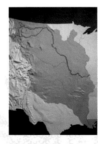

© Thinkstock

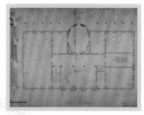

Washington: President's House (plan), 1792, by James Hoban. *Thomsas Jefferson Papers: An Electronic Archive*. Boston, Mass.: Massachusetts Historical Society, 2003

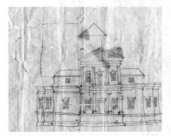

Jefferson's sketch of Monticello I or first house.
© Thomas Jefferson Foundation in Monticello

American Treasures of the Library of Congress, Library of Congress. "Jefferson's Recipe for Vanilla Ice Cream." 1780's

© Thinkstock

Garden Book, 1776-1824, page 30, *Thomsas Jefferson Papers: An Electronic Archive*. Boston, Mass.: Massachusetts Historical Society, 2003

West Virginia: The Rand-McNally Vest pocket map of West Virginia, showing all counties, cities, towns, railways, lakes, rivers, etc. G3891.P3 1908. R2. Special Collections, University of Virginia, Charlottesville, VA

Library Elevation of the Rotunda. A Calendar of the Jefferson papers of the University of Virginia. Jefferson Papers. Special Collections, University of Virginia, Charlottesville, VA

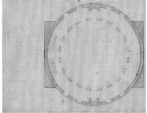

The Rotunda. A Calendar of the Jefferson papers of the University of Virginia. Jefferson Papers. Special Collections, University of Virginia, Charlottesville, VA

© Thinkstock

© Thinkstock

Dawson's Row
University of Virginia Visual History Collection. RG-30/1/10.011. Special Collections, University of Virginia, Charlottesville, VA

University of Virginia Visual History Collection. RG-30/1/10.011. Special Collections, University of Virginia, Charlottesville, VA

Jefferson's grave marker
© Thomas Jefferson Foundation at Monticello, photograph by Mary Porter

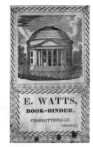

E. Watts, book-binder, Charlottesville, Virginia. Broadside 1827 .E15. Special Collections, University of Virginia, Charlottesville, VA

View of the University of Virginia, Charlottesville and Monticello, taken from Lewis Mountain
University of Virginia Visual History Collection. RG-30/1/10.011. Special Collections, University of Virginia, Charlottesville, VA

University of Virginia
University of Virginia Visual History Collection. RG-30/1/10.011. Special Collections, University of Virginia, Charlottesville, VA

University of Virginia Rotunda Fire
Holsinger Studio Collection, ca. 1890-1938, Accession #9862, Special Collections, University of Virginia, Charlottesville, VA

Historical Photo Credits

These images appear on pages 35–82.

University of Virginia Rotunda Dome Room
Holsinger Studio Collection, ca. 1890-1938,
Accession #9862, Special Collections, University
of Virginia, Charlottesville, VA

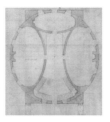

The Rotunda first floor plan. A
Calendar of the Jefferson papers of
the University of Virginia. Jefferson
Papers. Special Collections, University
of Virginia, Charlottesville, VA

© Thinkstock

A new and historical map of Albemarle County,
Virginia. G3883 .A3 1907 .M3. Special Collections,
University of Virginia, Charlottesville, VA

A new and historical map of Albemarle County, Virginia.
G3883 .A3 1907 .M3. Special Collections, University of
Virginia, Charlottesville, VA

West Virginia: The Rand-McNally Vest pocket map
of West Virginia, showing all counties, cities, towns,
railways, lakes, rivers, etc. G3891.P3 1908. R2. Special
Collections, University of Virginia, Charlottesville, VA

Ednam in Albemarle County
Holsinger Studio Collection, ca. 1890-1938, Accession #9862,
Special Collections, University of Virginia, Charlottesville, VA

Ednam in Albemarle County
Holsinger Studio Collection, ca. 1890-1938,
Accession #9862, Special Collections,
University of Virginia, Charlottesville, VA

John Rogan at the Boar's Head Inn site
Rip Payne Collection, Albemarle Charlottesville
Historical Society.

Jane Haley/University of Virginia Public Affairs

Aerial view of Monticello Vegetable
Garden, Vineyard, and South
Orchard © Thomas Jefferson
Foundation at Monticello,
photograph by Leonard Phillip

Jane Haley/University of Virginia Public Affairs

Dan Addison/University of Virginia Public Affairs

© Thinkstock

© Thinkstock

© Thinkstock

Dan Addison/University of Virginia Public Affairs

Garden Book, 1776-1824, page 30 and 31, *Thomsas Jefferson Papers: An Electronic Archive*. Boston, Mass.: Massachusetts Historical Society, 2003

Jane Haley/University of Virginia Public Affairs

Dan Addison/University of Virginia Public Affairs

Dan Addison/University of Virginia Public Affairs

Cole Geddy/University of Virginia Public Affairs

Aerial view of Monticello Vegetable Garden, Vineyard, and South Orchard
© Thomas Jefferson Foundation at Monticello, photograph by Leonard Phillip

Additional Photo Credits
See page 2.